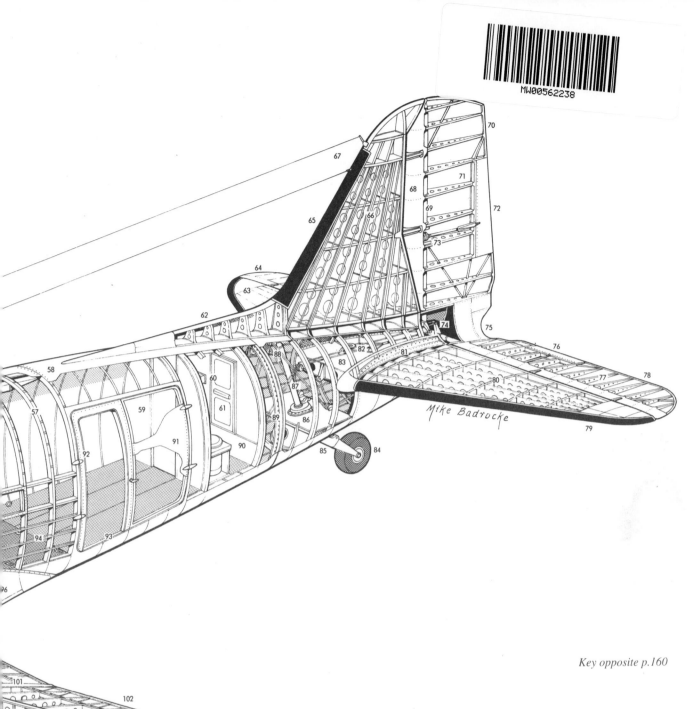

67

70

68

71

69

72

65

66

73

64

63

75

62

74

76

58

88

82

81

57

59

83

80

77

78

60

87

91

61

86

79

89

85

84

90

Mike Badrocke

92

Key opposite p.160

93

94

96

101

102

103

104

14

113

112

111

110

109

108

105

107

106

SIXTY GLORIOUS YEARS

SIXTY GLORIOUS YEARS

A Tribute to the Douglas DC-3 Dakota

ARTHUR PEARCY

Motorbooks International
Publishers & Wholesalers ®

This edition first published in 1995 by Motorbooks International,
Publishers & Wholesalers, PO Box 2, 729 Prospect Avenue,
Osceola, WI 54020, USA.

© 1995 by Arthur Pearcy

Previously published by Airlife Publishing Ltd, Shrewsbury, England, 1995

Library of Congress Cataloging-in-Publication Data is available

ISBN 0-7603-0192-1

Printed and bound in Singapore by Kyodo Printing Co. (S'pore) Pte Ltd

Contents

John C. Brizendine

Joined Douglas Aircraft Company, Santa Monica, California in August 1950.
Completed 33 years with Douglas/McDonnell Douglas.
President of Douglas Aircraft Company component of McDonnell Douglas from 1973 to end of 1982.

Foreword

Two milestones in the annals of aviation will be celebrated in 1995: six decades of service by the world's most enduring transport aircraft design, the DC-3; and the 75th anniversary of the founding of the DC-3's designer, developer, and producer, the Douglas Aircraft Company. It is not surprising, then, that our esteemed author would be found with his publisher arranging yet another literary salute to "The Grand 'Ole Lady".

It is fitting that Arthur Pearcy should author this Celebration, for he is probably the most knowledgeable person alive in DC-3 lore...her history, her exploits, and her enduring contributions to the betterment of mankind.

It has been said, when referring to significant happenings, that "timing is everything." While it may be argued that this adage is somewhat an over-statement, there is little doubt about the importance in its underlying implication.

The emergence of the DC-3 in 1935 was an event that was "ready to happen"... that is, all of the necessary ingredients for a successful breakthrough in air transportation had converged at the right time, in the right place, with the right people in the right environment.

The state-of-the-art — that body of technical knowledge and know-how to effectively employ it — had reached a "critical mass." Engine development had progressed sufficiently to provide adequate power with acceptable efficiency, durability, and reliability. The variable pitch propeller likewise enhanced aircraft performance. Strong, light-weight aluminium alloys with well known physical properties were available. And the monocoque structural design and construction techniques had been developed and proven to yield further weight reduction and operating efficiency.

From the business enterprise perspective, strong demand existed for safer, faster, more reliable and lower cost air transportation. An aircraft which could carry enough passengers at low enough operating cost to produce a profit for the airlines would certainly find a ready market. And such market demand would likely provide acceptable financial risk for the investors.

Finally, the catalyst to bring all of these ingredients together existed in an extraordinary team of people who constituted the Douglas Aircraft Company, Inc. Brilliantly led by its founder Donald Wills Douglas, the DACo, then in its 15th year as a full service aircraft developer and builder, had some notable achievements already distinguishing its reputation...for example, the first airplane to lift a useful load greater than its own empty weight ("The Cloudster", circa 1921; the "First Around the World" flight (Douglas "World Cruisers", 1924); The Collier Trophy award 1 July, 1935 (for DC-1 and DC-2 development).

The DC-3 was created from the visions and specifications, skills and dedication, integrity and commitment of a relatively small band of people. They represented both sides of the buyer-seller and user-producer equations, where a unique and lasting synergism existed. A man's word was his bond; trust was both earned and given.

The DC-3 was the product of all the above. Its "timing was right", and as history of the ensuing decades has shown, its timing may have been Providential.

Donald Douglas' leadership and personal intregrity never faltered as the decades passed. I shall not forget witnessing an event almost 30 years after the DC-3 began her pre-eminent reign. Donald Douglas and C.E. Woolman, then Chairman of Delta Air Lines, were discussing the need for a new airplane (possibly a "DC-3 replacement"?) Mr. Woolman said to Mr. Douglas, "Doug, if you will build it we will buy it". To which Mr. Douglas responded, "C.E. if you will buy it, we will build it." It was a deal: the two long-time friends shook hands and the DC-9 was launched.

The "Right Stuff" has been around for a long, long time!

John C. Brizendine

Acknowledgements

All the words available, including comparable, immortal, ubiquitous etc. translated into many languages have been used to exhaustion for 60 years to describe this unique transport – the DC-3. Any tribute such as this volume could never have been accomplished single-handed and since the 'A' Team commenced research into the DC-3, many years ago, the list of friends world-wide has grown. Many are now very personal friends who we visit whenever possible and their talent is included in this tribute.

As usual and very appropriate, my first and most sincere thanks must go to the Douglas Aircraft Company, and the many personnel past and present who, over the years since the 1960s, have not only made us welcome at the Long Beach facility, but who have offered every encouragement for any projected volume on Douglas products which we have ever suggested.

Over the many years in office, friend Harry Gann as the company archivist has provided hundreds of photographs. Even though retired, Harry has been rehired in this the 75th anniversary year of the company. Another good friend, Don Hanson, Director Media Relations, hosted us on many of our visits and succumbed to our every need. His professional prompting and acknowledgement has been most encouraging.

John C Brizendine befriended us whilst he was serving as President of the Douglas Aircraft Company at Long Beach from 1973 to the end of 1982. Now retired, John kindly consented to write the Foreword for this volume for which we are most grateful. It is coincidental that the 60th anniversary of the DC-3 should fall in the same year as the 75th anniversary of the forming of the Douglas Aircraft Company. Much has transpired since then and John Brizendine has been very involved with later developments, especially with the most successful DC-9 series which has today developed into another generation of high quality products from the Long Beach facility. We now have in service the MD-80 and MD-90 series of airliners putting the company at the forefront of commercial aviation in the world.

Many friends old and new have kindly contributed to this Diamond Anniversary tribute to the DC-3. These include Peter M Bowers; William T Larkins; Boardman C Reed; Jay Wright; Edward J Davies; Jimmy Davidson; Henry M Holden; Mark Yokers; (USA). Michael Prophet; Ron Mak; Coert Munk; (The Netherlands). J.M. Gradidge; Frank & Michael Hudson; Mike Hooks; Peter R Arnold; Jerry Scutts; Alec Thompson: (United Kingdom). Jan Stroomenbergh; Fred Prior; (Canada). Petur P Johnson (Iceland).

The DC-3 operators who kindly contributed include Paul L Freeston; Andrew Breedon; (Air Atlantique). Peter Vincent of Vincent Aviation (New Zealand); Richard Branson (Vintage Airways) Florida. Milo Kalberer (Classic Air) Switzerland. HQ South African Air Force in Pretoria. Edith Salerno (SALAIR) in the USA.

No acknowledgement would be complete without a mention of the Airlife Publishing Limited team headed by Alastair Simpson, Managing Director, with Peter Coles as Editor-in-Chief and Anne Cooper who knows just where to channel any problems. To all at Longden Road, Shrewsbury my heartfelt thanks. Last but not least to the other half of the "A" Team, my wife Audrey who proof reads and is a source of encouragement. Thank you all.

My sincere apologies for any DC-3 nut I have not mentioned, but who contributed to this volume. The words of Teilhard-du-Chardin aptly describe the DC-3. "I am a pilgrim of the future on the way forward from a journey made through the wisdom of the past."

April 1995. Sharnbrook
Bedfordshire

Author's Notes

History is always studied after the fact. It just cannot be otherwise. Sometimes during long periods of reflection this study elicits regret or sorrow, and more often, nostalgia. When a Douglas DC-3 is seen on the ground or in the air, history immediately comes up and slaps one in the face. There is no remorse here – it is more than a refreshing sight to see.

In this day of disposable consumables with planned obsolescence, it is a refreshing sight to see such an old veteran in all its spendour. The Grand 'Ole Lady will celebrate her 60th birthday on Sunday 17 December 1995 and this, the Model T of aviation is still around, albeit in smaller numbers. There is very little controversy when pilots talk about the airplane that shaped the world of aviation.

A quick look at the Bibliography at the rear of this volume signifies not only the popularity of the DC-3, but also the volume of tasks it has undertaken over six decades. In this respect it has been nigh impossible to record all its achievements in this pictorial tribute. Two examples spring to mind – the involvement in Malaya during "Operation Firedog" which commenced in June 1948 involving Dakotas operating as 'Voice' aircraft in a long twelve years of a battle against communist terrorists. Earlier "Operation High Jump" took six US Navy R4D-transports to Antarctica being launched from the carrier USS *Philippine Sea* (CVA-47) on 29 January 1947. This led to the Douglas transport continuing to operate in the sub-zero temperatures for progressive years under "Operation Deep Freeze".

After six decades most DC-3s have undergone modification of some sort. One pilot, employed in hauling cargo told us that he can fly a different registered DC-3 each day of the week, and all different in some respect. The transport changes hands quite rapidly so that civil registers are out of date as soon as they are published. The FAA DC-3 register in the USA is a good example. The market for military air arm transports (C-47 Skytrains) is not so flexible, but any transports that become surplus are much sought after on the civil market. Their maintenance and condition is normally impeccable, often with low flying hours and the sale including spares, especially if the type is being phased out.

It was a pleasant surprise to have confirmation from our old friend, Don Hanson, Director Media Relations, with the Douglas Aircraft Company, that Air Atlantique based here in the UK at Coventry, possibly has the largest fleet of civil operated DC-3s in the world with eleven on the current inventory with 35 out of their 45 active pilots rated on the Dakota.

A recent photo depicting a South African Air Force turboprop VIP Dakota, one of their fleet of 40 plus still in service, is a reminder that the DC-3 has been used in a VIP configuration for many years, commencing possibly with the C-41 (DC-3-253) used by General 'Hap' Arnold as early as 1938. For many years the Thai Royal family used a VIP C-47 transport fitted with a luxurious interior. Early in 1961, two RAF Dakotas were chosen and operated by the Queen's Flight in the Nepalese sector of the Asian tour undertaken by HM Queen Elizabeth and the Duke of Edinburgh. They were considered to be the most suitable and proven type for the conditions involved. The airfield at Kathmandu, on the Royal route, was the only airfield in Nepal with an all-weather runway 800 yards long and about 4,000 feet above mean sea level (AMSL). During World War 2 the Douglas transport was so popular and versatile that most high-ranking officers sought to use the type, often as a very personal transport with a luxurious interior. Likewise after World War 2 high ranking company executives chose the DC-3 as an executive transport fitted out with the latest weather radar and avionics.

It is highly recommended that any student of aviation transport through the early years reads a copy of *Douglas Propliners DC-1 to DC-7* which is now available.

The first flight of the first DC-3, a DST-114, X14988, was from Clover Field, Santa Monica at 1500 hours on 17 December 1935 with Carl Cover – Douglas vice-president of sales – as pilot, accompanied by two flight engineers, Ed Stineman and Frank Collbohm, and by Jack Grant, mechanic. The flight lasted 30 min and was followed by two more to bring the total time that day to 1 hr 40 min. Depicted parked at Clover Field during 1935 is X14988 c/n 1494 later registered NC14988 for American Airlines. *(William T Larkins)*

Introduction

Sixty years ago one of aviation's most enduring legends was born. On that day – 17 December 1935 – the Douglas DC-3 made her first flight. For one hour and 40 minutes she was airborne, initiating a flying career that has made her the best known airplane of all times.

The ability of the DC-3 to survive potentially catastrophic circumstances in both commercial and military service and her continuing longevity, which has reached far beyond that expected of a machine, have nurtured the legend about this twin-engined transport.

But in December 1935 in Santa Monica, California, no one at the Douglas Aircraft Company could anticipate the fame the DC-3 would attain. In fact, in contrast to the maiden flights of today's new aircraft, the flight from Clover Field aroused little, if any, excitement.

Frank Collbohm, then flight test engineer at Douglas was aboard the DC-3 and recalls the flight was 'rather routine'. And indeed it was, for company executives did not walk out to the nearby runway to watch the historic take-off. Apparently not a single photograph was taken of the event, for none can be found in the company archives.

But as the DC-3 and its many military counterparts, the C-47, C-53 and R4D-, went into service in increasing numbers, their performance was anything but routine. Durable and dependable, the DC-3 quickly revolutionised commercial air travel. She became the first aircraft that could make money for its operators just by hauling passengers.

It was this performance, plus her spectacular ability to stay in the air when lesser airplanes fell to the ground and to take-off with overloads that astounded her designers that helped to stimulate the DC-3 legend.

From World War 2 came a multitude of DC-3 stories. She became a favourite in dispatches from war correspondents. Poems and songs were written about her. General Dwight D. Eisenhower characterised her as one of the four weapons that helped the most to win the war. After the war, thousands of surplus C-47s converted to airline use put civil aviation back into business. To countless thousands of travellers, the DC-3 was the airplane in which they made their first flight.

The DC-3 pioneered such advances in passenger comfort as the heated cabin and sound proofing; for the pilot there were powered brakes, constant speed propellers and an autopilot; and the airlines received the first airplane that reduced the United States coast-to-coast time to 15 hours, a considerable improvement over existing equipment.

The first DC-3 built was designated "DST" (Douglas Sleeper Transport), designed in response to a request for an "Air Pullman" from Cyrus R. Smith and Bill Littlewood from American Airlines to Donald W. Douglas, founder of the Douglas company. Fourteen berths were installed in the cabin.

It soon developed, however, that the widened fuselage required for the berths was more important to the airlines than providing the luxury of slumber, for, minus the berths, the DC-3 'Day Plane' could accommodate 20 to 30 seats, a significant increase over the capacities of airliners then in service.

Mr Donald W Douglas when honorary chairman of the McDonnell Douglas board of directors, in noting the 40th anniversary of the DC-3, declared:

"I do not believe that any of us who worked on the design and development of the DC-1 and DC-2 quite realised at the time that we were really building the DC-3, an airplane that would outlast the careers of us all. I think it is well we remember that it was the skill, the courage and faith of the flyers themselves who made the DC-3 great. To paraphrase 'Ole Man River,' the DC-3 flies on and on. And who knows? Perhaps she will fly on forever. I hope she does."

This was the 103rd production DC-3 and the third to be registered in Britain. Assembled by Fokker as a DC-3-194C on 27 August 1937 for KLM PH-ARB *Buizerd* escaping to the UK in May 1940 and registered G-AGBD to KLM on 29 July 1940. Used by BOAC and went to the Royal Netherland Air Force in 1945. To KLM as PH-TBD on 16 December 1945, and to Skyways as G-AGBD *Sky Hawk* on 1 August 1946. Operated by BOAC in 1952 followed by various owners and last owner reported as Ethiopian Airlines. Photo's show the passenger door on the starboard side. *(AP Publications)*

Into Service and War Clouds

The DC-3 was not only bigger than the DC-2 but also much easier and safer to fly. The automatic pilot, then only recently developed by the Sperry Gyroscope Company, was installed as standard equipment. Two sets of instruments were installed in the cockpit, each independent of the other; if one set went unserviceable the other was there for an emergency. Because the airlines were beginning to go in for night flights, special lights to illuminate the instrument panel were designed. So excellent was the design that the basic specifications for the aircraft were never changed – a rare thing in aviation. The DC-3 was an immediate success.

The first American Airlines DC-3 went into service on 7 June 1936 on the non-stop New York to Chicago route. Orders poured in from other US and foreign airlines. The speed with which the airline industry converted to DC-3s seemed limited only by the rate at which Douglas could produce them at Santa Monica.

Not only was the DC-3 larger, faster, and more luxurious than any previous aircraft, but it was also more economical to operate. Standardisation on the DC-3 reduced maintenance and other costs and boosted safety records.

Within a few months of the DC-3's introduction into scheduled service the president of United Air Lines, W.A. Patterson, was forced to admit that the days of their Boeing 247s were numbered. The new DC-3 was knocking 60 minutes off the journey time, making money as fast as the 247s lost it. United purchased a new fleet of DC-3s powered by Pratt & Whitney engines, the first going into service on 30 June 1937. It was not long before the airline had figures on the profit side of their ledger.

Three years to the day, on Wednesday 1 July 1936, after the DC-1 had made its first flight, the DC-3 received recognition as the "outstanding twin-engined commercial transport plane." Those were the words that President Roosevelt read from the citation when he presented Donald W. Douglas with the Collier Trophy at the White House. "This airplane," the script recounted, "by reason of its high speed, economy, and quiet passenger comfort, has been generally adopted by transport lines throughout the USA. Its merit has been further recognised by its adoption abroad, and its influence on foreign design is already apparent. In making this award, recognition is given to the technical and production personnel of the Douglas organisation."

When the attack on Pearl Harbor came on 7 December 1941, the first US airline to get involved was obviously Pan American who had begun a scheduled service to Khartoum on 21 October 1941, as envisaged in a Presidential directive covering the delivery of Lend-Lease aircraft. US Ferry Command began services from Bolling Field, Washington DC. to Cairo, Egypt on 14 November, the route being extended to Basra a few weeks later. On the day of the Japanese attack, Western Airlines had its Douglas DC-3s requisitioned to fly desperately needed ammunition to the US west coast. Five days later, the Assistant Secretary of War and Gen Arnold directed Ferry Commands Col Olds to call on the airlines for the transport of vital men and materials. The first agreement was made with Pan American on the following day, to extend its African service to Teheran with the further prospect of an extension to the USSR. On 14 December American Airlines took part in a copybook exercise when the War Department called the ATA and asked for the immediate and secret movement of troops to a destination in South America. Pilots on flights were ordered to land at the nearest airport and discharge passengers. The DC-3 transports were then flown to a secret US Army base and 15 aircraft loads of troops were flown to Brazil.

RIGHT:
Japan made early use of both the DC-2 and DC-3 airliners, purchasing a single DC-2 followed by five unassembled aircraft. The DC-3 followed with 20 delivered as parts, followed by two DC-3As. Greater Japan Air Lines of Tokyo was formed in August 1939 by the reorganisation of Japan Air Lines, ceasing operations on 24 August 1945. Seen parked at Tokyo is their second DC-3 J-BDOL which unfortunately is not identified. *(AP Publications)*

LEFT:

Very rare photo showing a KLM DC-3 PH-ASK c/n 2036 delivered via Fokker on 9 April 1938 and named *Kemphaan* parked at Oslo on 9 April 1940 with Luftwaffe aircraft in the background. It was captured by the Germans at Oslo but released to fly back to Schiphol as the Netherlands was still neutral. However it was captured again by the Germans at Schiphol when they invaded on 16 May 1940. It was given Luftwaffe markings 'NA+LB' for ferry flight to Berlin-Staaken airfield. On 18 June 1940 registered D-AOFS and operated by Lufthansa. All the neutral European countries carried identification in large letters below and above the aircraft as seen on PH-ASK. *(Merle Olmsted Collection)*

ABOVE:

Most of these early Long Beach built C-47-DL transports were delivered in mid-1942 and are depicted during early airborne forces exercises. The first two Skytrains on the left of the photo – 41-18415 c/n 4477 and 41-18472 c/n 4564 are still flying today. Prior to the tragedy of Pearl Harbor a large number of Douglas twin-engined transports were on order. This included 545 C-47s in September 1940 and 92 C-53 Skytroopers in mid-1941 as well as a further 200 C-47s. *(Douglas)*

Busy scene at BOAC's wartime base located at Whitchurch, Bristol with BOAC DC-3s and other camouflaged airliners parked. The DC-3 with its engines being ground tested is DC-3-194C PH-ARB of KLM *Buizerd* delivered from Fokker on 27 August 1937 and escaping to the United Kingdom during the German invasion of the Netherlands in May 1940. On 29 July 1940 it was allocated G-AGBD with the Royal Dutch airline and was used by BOAC. After World War 2 in 1945 it went to the Royal Netherland Air Force as 'NL202' with 1316 Comm Flight prior to returning to KLM initially as G-AGBD then PH-TBD. The DC-3 later served in the United Kingdom with Skyways and BOAC. Its c/n was 1980. *(IWM)*

Scene at Budapest Airport, Hungary during 1941 with a Lufthansa DC-3-220B assembled by Fokker D-AAIG c/n 2095 being prepared for an internal flight. The airliner was delivered on 11 January 1939 going to Ceskoslovenska Latecka Spolecnost (CLS) in Czechoslovakia as OH-AIG later D-AAIG when the Germans invaded, going to Lufthansa on 24 July 1940. The DC-3 crashed in the sea near Frederikstad, Norway on 21 April 1944. It was 1938 when the Germans overran Czechoslovakia with the complete DC-3 fleet of CLS taken over by Tschechische Luftverkehr Gesellschaft with three registered with Deutsche Luft Hansa (DLH). Through neutral sources DLH kept their Douglas transports modified with all changes recommended by the manufacturer and Civil Aeronautics Board during World War 2. *(Heinz J Nowarra)*

BELOW:
Passengers seen disembarking from Fokker assembled DC-3-214 SE-BAA *Ornen* c/n 1947 delivered on 10 June 1947 going to Swedish Air Lines the following month. It survived World War 2 going to the Scandinavian Airlines System (SAS) as *Arne Viking* on 1 August 1948. In December 1953 it went as SE-BWE to Transair-Sweden and on 21 February 1961 joined the United Nations Organisation (UNO) in the Congo, registered UN-216. *(AP Publications)*

During World War 2 the Swedish airline ABA tried to maintain its neutrality and most of its pre-war airline services with great difficulty. For all wartime flights the fleet of five DC-3s were clearly marked as depicted in this photo with 'SWEDEN' in large letters on the fuselage and underneath. On 28 May 1943 SE-BAF c/n 2133 a DC-3-268 *Gladan* was shot down over the North Sea whilst en-route from the United Kingdom to Sweden. After this incident the remaining airliners were given an overall orange colour scheme. In addition to 'SWEDEN' 'SCHWEDEN' was also applied. *(SAS)*

RIGHT:

The influence of both KLM and Fokker in the Netherlands on the DC-2 and DC-3 airliner gave that country, and indeed Europe, an important role in the development of the types. Although never built by Fokker, despite having a licence, most of those supplied pre-war to Europe were assembled at Schiphol and KLM became one of the major users until 1940. Another claim to fame was the excellent performance of the DC-2 PH-AJU in coming in first in the transport section of the England to Australia air race of 1934, and second overall. Today the Dutch Dakota Association (DDA) has two DC-3s and one DC-2 on its inventory. Depicted is a DC-3 being shipped for KLM during 1937 via the canal system in the Netherlands.

(Peter M. Bowers Collection)

LEFT:
The pilot of C-47 Skytrain *The Galloping Goose* Lt. Bill Andrews is seen sat astride the port Pratt & Whitney Twin Wasp engine which carries the name of his sweetheart Edna. Photo taken at Del Valle army air base, Texas during September 1942, prior to 52 Douglas C-47s from the four squadrons comprising the 316th Troop Carrier Group departing for the Middle East to support the Allied advance in North Africa. *(AP Publications)*

BELOW:
CLS – Ceskoslovenska Latecka Spolecnost of Prague purchased both the DC-2 and DC-3 via Fokker agency before World War 2. They were operated on scheduled services within Europe until 1938 when the airline was taken over by Germany and the airliners re-registered from 'OK' registration to 'D' and operated by Lufthansa. Depicted at Prague are seven DC-3s D-AAIG c/n 2095: D-AAIE c/n 2023: D-AAIF c/n 2024: D-AAIH c/n 1973: D-AAIG c/n 2095: D-AAIO c/n 1582 and D-AAIB c/n 1582. An additional DC-3 was D-AAID c/n 1565. *(AP Publications)*

In 1933 it was TWA who commenced the DC-3 story by ordering the DC-1. The DC-2 followed and the first DC-3s were delivered in April 1937 and the type continued in use with the airline throughout World War 2. By 1946 there were no less than 76 of the type in the TWA fleet, the last being sold in 1957. Depicted is a typical prewar airline scene with both mail and parcels being loaded into the front cargo compartment of a TWA DC-3. *(AP Publications)*

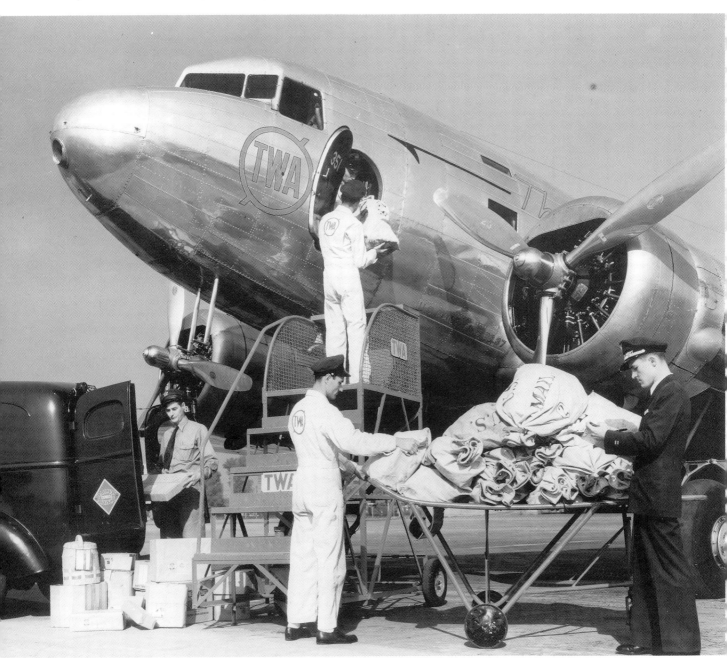

This Trans Continental & Western Air – TWA – DC-3B-202 NC17313 c/n 1923 was delivered on 1 May 1937 and is depicted parked at the Union Air Terminal, Los Angeles in 1939 being readied for a transcontinental flight to the east coast. By October 1941 this airliner was with Pan Am in Africa, becoming a C-49D 42-38256 on 14 March 1942. As LR233 it went to the RAF on 1 April 1942 becoming 'H-Harry' with No.31 Squadron in India. It was finally struck off charge on 25 October 1942 at Dinjan after being grounded for a Wright Cyclone engine change. *(AP Publications)*

Ramp scene at the Oklahoma City factory September 1944 with a batch of newly built C-47B-5-DK Skytrains parked destined for delivery flight to the USSR and awaiting ferry pilots. Skytrain 43-48752 c/n 14568/26013 is from a batch of ten delivered on 16 September and the factory batch of 349 transports 43-48563 to 43-48912 under Contract AC-46652 included transports destined for the USAAF, US Navy, Russia, RAF, RAAF and RNZAF. Over 700 Douglas C-47 transports were delivered to Russia under Lend-Lease agreement. *(Douglas)*

Factory Production

The parent factory at Santa Monica, California, had grown up over the years. It had continually expanded since the time it was built during the Golden Years of aviation, prior to the great Depression in the United States. In 1939 the factory was clogged with production contracts for commercial, military and new Lend-Lease aircraft contracts. The airfield at the factory for conducting test flights was beginning to be too small for fast attack bombers such as the A-20 Boston. It was these obvious deficiencies that required that the C-47 programme be conducted with plant facilities entirely new in concept. For an increased tempo in production, the need for interchangeability of assemblies and parts, made it mandatory that steel production tooling and assembly jigs be designed and built. Space was at a premium in the parent plant. The whole concept of production tooling had to be radically improved to accomplish mass output of assemblies to the aircraft production line, and subsequently the flight line. It would have been foolhardy to expect that the parent factory could produce the C-47 in quantities desired with the existing facilities. The Douglas El Segundo Division was busy with the production of the SBD- Dauntless and could not therefore function as a feeder facility for the C-47 programme.

Santa Monica was retained and produced the C-53 Skytrooper, the C-54 Skymaster and the A-20. The first C-53 was 41-20045 c/n 4810 delivered on 5 October 1941. After World War 2 Santa Monica built the Super DC-3. The production graph for the Douglas factories indicates that between October/December 1941 Santa Monica produced 32 C-53 Skytroopers whilst between January/March 1942 Long Beach delivered 41 C-47 Skytrains. The factory programme was complicated being supplanted by the Reconstruction Finance Corporation (RFC) and its subsidiary the Defense Plant Corporation which built numerous wartime factories. One of these was located at Oklahoma City and was used only for the C-47 Skytrain and the C-117 transport. Lots of Skytrain orders were cancelled at the end of World War 2 and in any case the lease then expired. It was 1943 before the first Oklahoma City build C-47-DK was completed and between July/September that year a total of 95 Skytrain transports were completed. On 24 July 42-92092 c/n 11854 was the first.

The earliest C-47 Skytrains were the Long Beach C-47-DLs which had a 12-volt electric system. These were followed by 2,954 C-47A-DLs which had a 24-volt system to cope with the greater electrical demand. Block numbers were allocated as improvements were incorporated within the basic C-47A airframe. These included equipment changes and some modifications which were incorporated in the field. With further orders for the transport 2,300 more C-47A-DKs came off the Oklahoma City line. These were virtually identical to the Long Beach models. The C-47A was followed by the C-47B from both plants, this model being designed for high altitude operation over the 'Hump' route into China on the India-China sector and had the more powerful Pratt & Whitney R-1830-90C supercharged engine, cabin fuel tanks, hot air heating and a greater all-up weight of 30,000 lb (13,600 kg). These superchargers were often removed post-war to make the C-47D, but the US Army added them again for high altitude flight tests on equipment, and one skydiving DC-3 owner fitted his aircraft with larger Pratt & Whitney R-1830-75 engines which assisted the climb to height.

The full story of C-47 production and the techniques that were involved would fill a large volume. A look at the quarterly summary of deliveries reveals that the busiest period was the quarter April/June 1944 when a total of 1,586 transports were produced, 698 at Long Beach, 539 at Oklahoma City, 48 for the US Navy, 218 for the RAF, seven for the RCAF, four for the RAAF, four for the South African Air Force, two for the RNZAF, four for China, three for the Netherlands East Indies Air Force (NEIAF) and 56 for Russia.

One of the most unusual derivatives of the 'Gooney Bird' was the XCG-17 experimental troop-transport glider. It was converted by removing the engines and fairing over the nacelles of a standard C-47-DL 41-18496 c/n 4588 at Clinton County Army airfield, Wilmington, Ohio in June 1944. Internally the cabin was lengthened six feet forward in order to accommodate 40 troops, or a pay load of 15,000 lb. It was a USAAF Wright Field project and first flight took place in June 1944. Some 400 lb of lead shot was added to the nose to ensure the glider was not tail heavy. It became the largest glider in the USA, carrying a payload of seven tons. It was later sold becoming a normal post-war DC-3 transport. *(Douglas)*

ABOVE:
Factory scene at Santa Monica as DC-3 airliners are complete and in the paint shop. Date is 6 October 1937. A look at the production listing for this period reveals five DC-3-228 for the Pan American Airways System, as depicted, and two for Panagra – Pan American Grace Airways Inc. Approximately every five days a new DC-3 was completed and ready for delivery. Sometimes the period was less. *(Douglas)*

LEFT:
Photos of Mr Donald W. Douglas with his factory products are comparatively rare. This photo depicts Donald Douglas deplaning from a new C-47 Skytrain, the major product of the Douglas Aircraft Company during World War 2. On his left is General George C. Marshall whilst on the right is an officer wearing a US 8th Air Force shoulder patch. *(Douglas)*

With wings and engines attached this photo depicts the Long Beach production line during February 1944 with C-47A-80-DL Skytrain transports nearing completion. The production line at this stage moved on rails fitted to the factory floor with the aircraft turned 30 degrees in order to conserve vital floor space. The records reveal that the majority of this batch of Skytrains were ferried to Europe during March and April 1944 in time for the invasion of Europe in June 1944. *(Douglas)*

The Long Beach factory in California produced a wartime grand total of 4,285 C-47 Skytrains for use by the Allies. This photo depicts the busy production line during November 1942 with a batch of C-47-DL transports well on the way to completion. The first three aircraft 41-18666/7/8 were ferried to the US 5th Air Force in Australia for use in the Pacific theatre of operations. They arrived in Australia in January 1943 so possibly went by sea. The Skytrain 41-18669 remained within the USA and survived World War 2. *(Douglas)*

Rework facilities were high on the list for routine maintenance for the many Skytrain transports operated by the USAAF and the US Navy during World War 2. The Pratt & Whitney R-1830-90 series of Twin Wasp engines were manufactured by the motor vehicle industry in the USA including Buick, Chrysler to name just two. Depicted is a crowded re-work facility for US Navy R4D-transports at Columbus, Ohio and operated by Curtiss-Wright. The outer wings of the transports have been temporarily removed to make more room.
(AP Publications)

2000th SKYTRAIN

On 2 October 1943 the Long Beach, California, factory completed the 2,000th C-47 Skytrain built at the plant. It was a C-47A-50-DL 42-24256 c/n 10118. Joe Messick, Public Relations Manager, was determined to make this roll-out a spectacular occasion with a double purpose in mind: it would be good publicity for the Douglas Aircraft Company, and it would give a huge boost to employee morale and incentive. When the Skytrain transport was rolled off the production line, the Douglas PRO Joe Messick autographed the fuselage. By the end of the work shift, hundreds of production workers had done the same thing. Although the chalk signatures and messages were rubbed off before the US Army Air Force would accept the transport, many

'Rosie Riveters' managed to get their names and addresses into the wheel wells and hidden compartments and thus started pen romances with the USAAF mechanics who discovered them much later. This C-47 Skytrain was one of seven assigned to the US 5th Air Force in Australia based then at Brisbane. Photo depicts the 2,000 C-47 on the flight line with 'Rosie Riveters' still chalking. Next to it is 42-24257 c/n 10119 whilst end of the line of transports is Skytrain 42-24243 c/n 10105 which went to the RAF as Dakota FL522 then to the South African Air Force as '6810'.

(Douglas Aircraft Company Press Release)

RIGHT:
During February 1943 the Douglas Aircraft Company Modification Center conceived a very unique variant of the C-47 Skytrain. This was the Douglas C-47C Waterbird or Dumbo as it was named unofficially. It was to be used for air-sea rescue operations in the Pacific fitted with two pontoons which were also used as fuel tanks containing fuel pumps and the aircraft's retractable landing gear. It weighed 34,162 lb with fuel and was powered by two Pratt & Whitney R-1830-92 engines that gave a top speed of 130 mph, some 30 mph slower than a conventional C-47. Seen in the factory at Oklahoma City is C-47C 42-92577 c/n 12393. Only five were built for use in the Pacific and in Alaska. *(Douglas)*

BELOW:
The prototype XC-47C floatplane was a Long Beach built C-47-DL 42-5671 c/n 7365 which first flew in July 1942. It was turned over to Edo for the installation of the amphibious kit. Flight tests were conducted at Floyd Bennett Field, New York with American Airlines at nearby La Guardia Field involved. The two pontoons were 41-foot long, and contained a series of watertight bulkheads and could carry fuel. Personnel from a wide variety of organizations were involved in this unique project. The USAAF at Wright-Patterson were heavily interested. This prototype was handed over to the USAAF on 26 January 1943 and on 13 November 1943 it crashed in Jamaica Bay, New York. *(Douglas)*

Inscribed 'Miscellaneous, veteran of SWPA' (South-west Pacific area) C-47-DL Skytrain 41-7732 c/n 4211 returns home to the Long Beach factory on 12 August 1944 covered in mission symbols and carrying the US 5th Air Force badge on the fin. It is depicted during a low flypast of the factory. Whilst in the Pacific it was allocated the radio call-sign 'VHCDL'. *(Douglas)*

WAR VETERAN

'THIS SHIP IS THE OLDEST, FASTEST C-47 IN THE SOUTHWEST PACIFIC, SO INTO WHOMSOEVER'S HANDS SHE FALLS, TREAT HER KINDLY AND SHE WILL ALWAYS GET YOU TO YOUR DESTINATION.'

The words above appeared on a plaque in *Miscellaneous* the twelfth C-47 Skytrain built for Uncle Sam and the first of many to join General George C. Kenney's Far East Air Forces. Built at Long Beach and delivered to the military on 13 February 1942. It went to Australia by surface freighter and was reassembled. By May it was on active service, transporting troops and supplies to the battle fronts, before returning to the USA on 12 August 1944 when it was retired with honors and participated in a nationwide bond tour. The Skytrain had flown more than 2,000 missions and close to 3,000 operational hours. She wore out 12 engines, had new wing tips, elevators, rudders all so frequently that pilots called her the 'ship worn angel.' C-47-DL 41-7732 c/n 4211. 5th Air Force Australia 14 April 1942.

(Press handout
Douglas Aircraft Company
August 1944)

The Royal New Zealand Air Force received its first Dakota under
Lend-Lease in February 1943 and by the end of 1945 a total of 49
had been delivered. Detached flights from No's 40 and 41 Squadrons
served in the forward areas in the Pacific theatre of operations. Five
were lost in accidents in 1945. Depicted unloading supplies at
Henderson Field, Guadalcanal during November 1943 is NZ3505 c/n
9422 ex C-47A-25-DL 42-23560 delivered 23 April 1943 and
assigned to No. 40 Squadron on 24 May. It was broken up in 1948.
(RNZAF)

South-west Pacific

The Pacific theatre of operations was vast and was divided into two theatres, the South-west Pacific Area involving Australia, New Guinea, Borneo, the Philippines, Java and part of the Solomons, all under General MacArthur, and the Pacific Ocean Area which included the North, Central and South Pacific under Admiral Nimitz. The US Army Forces HQ in the south Pacific at Suva in Fiji, moved to Noumea, New Caledonia at the end of July 1942. On 3 September 1942 the USAAF element in the South-west Pacific Area was constituted as the US 5th Air Force with HQ in Brisbane. The USAAF elements in the South Pacific Area became the US 13th Air Force on 13 January 1943 with HQ at Espiritu Santo, New Hebrides.

In Australia, the original transport element, the 21st and 22nd Troop Carrier Squadrons had a mixture of 32 Lockheed and Douglas aircraft, mainly KLM escapees from the East Indies as well as a few old Boeing B-17s and two Lockheed LB-30s. These were assigned to the Directorate of Air Transport. By September 1942 41 US aircraft out of 78 assigned were on hand but 15 were only fit to be used as spares. Two US Troop Carrier Squadrons of 13 C-47 Skytrains each were assigned, the first arriving in mid-October. The second was temporarily retained in the Pacific Ocean area and seven C-47s shuttled from Noumea to Guadalcanal for one month.

The 374th Troop Carrier Group was activated by the 5th Air Force to contain four squadrons and their first action was supply dropping in the Buna area of New Guinea during Operation 'Hatrack' in October 1942. They also flew in Australian troops to Wanigela airstrip in October/November, continuing landing or dropping supplies in the area until 23 January 1943 as well as evacuating casualties.

During January 1943, the 317th TCGrp flew 52 factory-new C-47 Skytrains from California to Australia. These were transferred to the 374th TCGrp and the 317th inherited the latter's weary mixture of C-47s, C-49s, and other types. By 30 June 1943 three and a half troop carrier groups were scheduled to be available, with a further group due in the third quarter of 1943. Control of the growing troop carrier element in Australia was carried out by the 54th Troop Carrier Wing constituted in February 1943. It functioned from Port Moresby in May 1943 and by the first week in July only the 37th TCGrp was assigned. At this time four new squadrons arrived, followed by two more soon after and another TCGrp following in September, to give a total of 14 squadrons.

During the Spring and early summer of 1943 the campaign in New Guinea steadily developed and a major base was developed at Dobodura, supplied solely by air. In June a further airfield was built at Tsili Tsili requiring 150 C-47 trips per day. This operation was largely unmolested by the Japanese, but on 15 July enemy fighters shot down two C-47s involved in moving the first fighter squadron ground crews into the field. Following a seaborne landing at Lae on 4 September 1943, 79 C-47s of the 54th TCWg flew 170 troops – US and Australian – across the 9,000 ft Owen Stanley mountains to a drop at Nadzab, 15 miles northwest of Lae to capture a site for an airfield and to cut off the Japanese at Salamaua. The airfield at Nadzab was in use on the following day and within ten days dispersals for 36 transports had been completed. Although Salamaua fell on 11 September, and Lae on the 16th, Nadzab was supplied by air for several months, continuing until the Lae-Nadzab road was completed in December 1943, with some 200 C-47 flights a day involved.

Subsequent operations in the capture of the Netherlands East Indies, Borneo etc were seaborne with C-47s only employed in landing troops, supplies and evacuating casualties. The 54th TCWg finally took overall command of 'Mission 75' in which 100 C-47 Skytrains and 272 C-46s together with 180 Douglas C-54s of Air Transport Command occupied Japan on 28 August 1945.

Despite the New Guinea natives being head-hunters, great interest was shown when the first USAAF C-47 Skytrain transports of the 5th Air Force arrived. This C-47 41-19472 c/n 6115 arrived in Australia on 7 January 1943. During Spring and early summer 1943, the New Guinea campaign steadily developed and a major air base was built at Tsili Tsili which catered for up to 150 C-47 flights a day. This operation was fortunately largely unmolested by the Japanese, but on 15 July 1943 enemy fighters shot down two C-47s involved in moving in ground crews for the first fighter squadron. *(Douglas)*

ABOVE:
Skytrain transports from a USAAF Troop Carrier Group are depicted parked on the dusty air strip located at Mokner, Black Island in Dutch New Guinea on 22 June 1944 during the Allied offensive against the Japanese. These transports took men and cargo to Allied bases on New Guinea, New Britain, Guadalcanal, and the Admiralty islands. Their headquarters were initially on New Guinea at Port Moresby, Finschhafen then Hollandia and finally to Leyte as the advance progressed. The first three Skytrains are '55' *The Pacemaker:* '61' *The Cherokee* and '68' *The Texan. (US Army)*

LEFT:
Spectacular photo depicting RNZAF Dakota NZ3517 c/n 12546 ex C-47A-10-DK 42-92715 from No.40 Squadron taking-off from the Piva jungle airstrip in Bougainville, Solomon Islands in the Pacific theatre of operations during January 1945. The red in the RNZAF national insignia was removed and a white bar added. This Dakota was broken up during 1948. *(RNZAF)*

Named *Jayhawk 2nd* this C-47 based in the Pacific theatre of operations has an aircraft wing section strapped under its fuselage. The Skytrain was an excellent workhorse and a jack of all-trades and became the world's most widely-used general-purpose military transport. It could transport a 7,500 lb cargo load or carry twenty-eight fully equipped troops. It could carry the wounded to base hospitals after being fitted with litters, carrying no less than twenty-four litter patients plus two nursing attendants. It had a combat radius of over 860 miles. *(Douglas)*

BELOW:
Photo taken at Nadzab, New Guinea on 11 September 1943 showing Allied personnel unloading vital supplies from C-47 Skytrains. Seven days earlier 79 C-47s of the 54th Troop Carrier Wing took 1,700 troops – US and Australian – across the 9,000 ft Owen Stanley mountains to drop at Nadzab, 15 miles north-west of Lae, to capture a site for an airfield in order to cut off the Japanese at Salamaua. The airstrip at Nadzab was in use the following day and within 10 days dispersals for 36 transports had been completed. Some 200 C-47 flights per day brought in vital supplies. *(US Air Force)*

Devastating scene at Yontan airport, Okinawa, after the Japanese made an attack with their special attack troops. At least ten of the attacking Japanese troop-laden aircraft were destroyed short of the target, six by US Marine Corps night fighters from the Second Marine Air Wing. Date of the attack was May 1945. Two USAAF Douglas transports are seen wrecked on the airport including C-54 Skymaster 42-72385 and in the foreground a Oklahoma City built C-47B-1-DK 43-48402 c/n 25663 delivered in August 1944.

(US Defense Dept. Marine Corps)

Troops of the Australian 2/16th Battalion arrive at Kaiapit by USAAF C-47 Skytrains on 21 September 1943 to begin their advance on foot along the Markham & Ramu Valleys. One of the six C-47s is a C-47A-5-DL 42-23353 '202' c/n 9215 delivered on 15 March 1943. The 374th Troop Carrier Group was activated by the US 5th Air Force with four squadrons. Their first action was '*Operation Hatrack*' in October 1942 supply dropping in the Buna area of New Guinea. They flew in Australian troops to Wanigela airstrip during October and November later flying in troops into Wau airstrip, New Guinea which had a 12 degree approach slope. Losses were surprisingly few. *(Australian War Memorial)*

BELOW:
Douglas C-47 Skytrain transports of the USAAF did a remarkable job keeping RAAF fighter squadrons supplied with fuel, stores and food whilst they operated in the Hollandia area of New Guinea. It was described as a giant taxi service. Depicted are a dozen transports from squadrons of the 317th Troop Carrier Group lined up ready for take-off after depositing drums of vital aviation fuel on the airstrip near Hollandia on 12 June 1944. The Group received Distinguished Unit Citations for its operations in New Guinea and the Philippines. *(RAAF)*

ABOVE:
Senior staff officers and staff from HQ 1st Australian Army await to emplane at Mareeba airstrip, Queensland, prior to flying to Port Moresby, New Guinea on 28 September 1944. The RAAF Dakota transport A65-4 is a Long Beach C-47-DL 42-32881 c/n 9107 delivered on 20 February 1943. It went to the RAAF on 26 March and to No. 36 Squadron coded 'RE-G' with radio-call-sign 'VH-CTD' on 11 May 1943. *(Australia War Memorial)*

LEFT:
Depicted is Dakota KN340 from No.243 Squadron 300 Wing based in Australia. Named *Spirit of Middlesex* it carried the radio call-sign 'VMYBM' and appropriately marked as the first British aircraft to land in Japan, at Atsugi, Tokyo in September 1945. It is an ex C-47D-25-DK 44-76323 c/n 32655 and plied between the many staging posts in the Pacific served by No.300 Wing which came under the command of the Admiral, British Pacific Fleet based at Leyte. *(R.C. Jones)*

HM King George VI followed by General Alexander, steps down from the VIP personal Dakota III FZ631 belonging to General Maitland Wilson and named *Freedom*. The date was 23 July 1944 and the place somewhere in Italy when a visit was made to British troops in the battlefield. The aircraft was a C-47A-1-DK 42-92392 c/n 12187. Today the main airframe and wing stubs are part of the DC-3 VH-BPA currently displayed on a pole at Cairns airport in Australia. *(PRB MoD)*

Middle East

Twenty million pounds of freight and war supplies were carried to the Russian, Mediterranean and Indian war fronts during 1943 by No.216 Group of RAF Transport Command based in the Middle East. Aircraft from the group also carried 100,000 passengers and 3,400,000 lb of mail. Casualties evacuated from the battlefields of the Western Desert, Sicily and Italy and the Dodecanese Islands totalled 16,400. To do all this, Dakotas and a variety of other aircraft from the group flew 70,000 hours and covered 10 million miles – forty times the distance to the moon.

Based in the Middle East since 1922 in the air transport role, No.216 Squadron flew DC-2K and DC-3 aircraft, re-equipping with Dakotas in 1943 while at Cairo West then known as LG224 or Kilo 26 on the road from Giza to Alexandria. Under the newly formed RAF Transport Command it began operating scheduled routes covering Egypt, Italy, West Africa, Iraq and Persia, but was heavily involved in the Western Desert. After the Salerno landings the squadron flew-in reinforcements and supplies. In the autumn it flew in support of the Aegean campaign dropping Greek paratroops it had assisted to train earlier in the year at No.4 Middle East Parachute Training School at Ramat David, near Haifa in Palestine.

On 30 April 1941 No.117 Squadron at Khartoum was formed from a detachment of No.216 Squadron it moving to Bilbeis – between Cairo and Alexandria – to train on DC-2K transports, later equipping with newly delivered Dakotas. Wherever the advancing troops went the Dakotas followed, ferrying stores, food and ammunition and evacuating the casualties – often under fire. Even before Sicily fell, a detachment of Dakotas was based at Catania.

During August 1942 No.267 Pegasus Squadron was based at Heliopolis when the first of three DC-3s allocated to the unit arrived. By September the squadron had moved to Bilbeis and was flying the Malta schedule, a typical sortie with DC-3 HK867 being recorded on 10 September. The transport was positioned at Shallufa, fully fuelled and heavily loaded for the flight to Luqa, departing late afternoon so as to pass Crete which was still occupied by the enemy, after dusk. Flight time was 8 hrs 45 mins. Cargo included one torpedo. After unloading, the DC-3 was refuelled and departed so as to be east of Crete by dawn, arriving at Cairo West 7 hrs 50 mins later.

The first Dakotas began to arrive in May 1943 being ferried via Takoradi and Cairo. Two of the unit's first transports were FD863 'A-Apple' and FD926 'B-Baker'. A detachment from No.267 followed the 8th Army to Tunis using the advanced base at Marble Arch, dropped paratroops in the invasion of Sicily, and landed on the beach-head in the invasion of Italy, with part of the squadron still maintaining the ever-lengthening supply line from Cairo West. By October the re-equipment with Dakotas was complete.

During the invasion of Sicily, the Dakotas moved men, light equipment for fighter squadrons, fighter wings and fighter control staffs, ammunition, a full headquarters consisting of over 100 personnel, and 40,000 lb of baggage and equipment, jeeps, motor-cycles, trailers, and casually filled a demand for 15 tons of boots and socks for the 7th Army. Altogether the Dakotas carried 763,230 lb of war supplies and evacuated 2,476 casualties. They flew 1,390 hours. The 'lifts' soared with the invasion of Italy to a total of 3,460,000 lb involving flights totalling 400,000 miles.

But this was only the beginning. The Italians capitulated and the 8th Army advanced so fast that the Desert Air Force decided to fly four more squadrons into the Taranto area immediately. The Dakotas carried 300 men and 100,000 lb of freight plus three RAF Regiment detachments complete with their guns to protect the airfields. For the next two and a half days the Dakotas flew in all the ammunition, petrol and rations that the squadrons needed – 250 tons in all.

ABOVE:
Skytrain C-47-DL 41-7845 c/n 4344 F for Freddy seen in flight in the Middle East. After completion at Long Beach on 28 April 1942 it arrived in the UK on 5 August joining the US 8th Air Force on 19 September. By 6 February 1943 it was based at Oran, Algeria, did survive World War 2 after service with the US 12th Air Force in Italy and was finally disposed of by the Foreign Liquidation Commission. *(IWM)*

RIGHT:
Douglas C-47 Skytrain transport seen in the Western Desert. It is from the 316th Troop Carrier Group which did sterling work supporting the British Eighth Army. On 11/12 December 1942 six transports from the 45th Squadron carried 11,664 gal of aviation fuel from a landing strip near Tobruk to an advanced airstrip returning with seventy-seven casualties. From 8 December 1942 to 24 January 1943 the group's aircraft carried more than 3,000,000 lb of freight including more than 500,000 gal of fuel and evacuated more than 1,400 casualties. In April they carried approximately 3,000,000 lb of freight and 7,000 passengers. *(IWM)*

LEFT:
The Commonwealth air forces were much in evidence in the Middle East theatre of operations. This photo depicts Royal Australian Air Force personnel sorting out vital rations just delivered to the airstrip by the RAF Dakota seen parked in the background. It had just arrived from Sicily to this forward base on the Italian mainland where these personnel formed part of a RAAF fighter-bomber squadron. *(RAAF)*

BELOW:
The 316th Troop Carrier Group with its four squadrons flew from Del Valle, Texas to Deversoir, Egypt in November 1942 equipped with 52 new C-47 Skytrains. It eventually moved with the British 8th Army to El Adem. Depicted in landing configuration is an early C-47-DL c/n 4473 delivered 28 June 1942, arriving in the Middle East theatre on 16 November, and by 11 June 1943 was based in Oran, Algeria. The Skytrain returned to the USA on 19 September 1945 and was sold to Brazil as PP-FVA prior to service with the Brazilian Air Force. It crashed at Natal on 25 March 1961. *(Peter M. Bowers)*

Depicted early in 1946 at Campoformido, Udine, Italy, is Dakota
KN452 c/n 32923 showing clearly the No.271 Squadron badge – a
gauntlet holding a red cross – a unit which operated from Down
Ampney, Gloucestershire for all the European airborne operations.
The transport used the radio call-sign 'ODVK' while in Italy. A C-53
Skytrooper is parked alongside. *(R. Bosley)*

RIGHT:
Skytrain 41-18456 'J for Johnny' c/n 4518 seen flying over mountain
terrain somewhere in Europe. It is from the 4th Troop Carrier
Squadron, 62nd Troop Carrier Group, which moved to the UK during
Aug/Sep 1942 being based at Keevil, Wiltshire prior to moving to
Tafaraoui, Algeria on 15 November 1942. It followed the battle-front
through North Africa to Sicily and Italy. The group was inactivated in
Italy on 14 November 1945. However 41-18456 returned to the US
on 30 January 1945. As CF-CUA it was destroyed by a time bomb at
St. Joachim, Province of Quebec on 9 September 1949.

Seen flying over the barren waste of Alaska is Long Beach built C-47A-35-DL 42-23805 c/n 9667 delivered on 10 June 1943. It is fitted with parapacks under the fuselage and under the centre wing sections. The structure of the C-47 Skytrain was very strong and the capability of the transport so versatile, far exceeding all expectations. Even bombs could be carried under the wings, airborne radar was fitted under the fuselage and in the nose. In South-East Asia Command – SEAC – spare C-47 wings are even strapped under the mainplane. *(William T. Larkins)*

Alaska

Because of its proximity to Japan via the Aleutian island chain, the possibility of a Japanese attack on Alaska was very real. As early as 27 February 1942 a Northwest Airlines DC-3 flew a survey flight to Alaska under government contract, to be later joined by DC-3s operated by Western and United Airlines. The threat was proved to be real when the Japanese attacked Dutch Harbor between 3/5 June 1942. By September 1942 Northwest was operating fifteen DC-3s on the run from Great Falls, Montana to Fairbanks, Alaska whilst Western had four DC-3s on the Ogden, Utah to Anchorage, Alaska run. When Lend-Lease deliveries to the USSR commenced during August 1942 the importance of Alaska was further increased. The Alaska Wing of the huge US Air Transport Command was formed with C-47 Skytrains on 17 October 1942.

The US 11th Air Force had one single squadron of C-47 Skytrains, namely the 42nd Troop Carrier Squadron by June 1942. The 54th TCSq joined it by August 1943 and between them their C-47s carried 7,500 tons of cargo and 15,000 men per month on intra-theatre flights, mainly to Attu, Adak and Shemya in the Aleutians. On behalf of ATC United Airlines operated the Anchorage to Adak shuttle at the request of the 11th Air Force, in September/October 1943. When there was a possibility that the 11th Air Force would lose its troop carrier squadrons in January 1944, Northwest Airlines began an Anchorage to Adak service with DC-3s, extended to Attu in July 1944. It was DC-3s and C-47s which bore the brunt of the work.

US Air Transport Command's north-west route extended for a distance of 2,210 statue miles from the domestic terminus at Great Falls, Montana, to Anchorage, Alaska. Great Falls itself was remote from the centres of aircraft production located in California and along the Atlantic seaboard. Between Great Falls and Anchorage, the route's major bases were at Edmonton in Alberta; Whitehorse in Yukon Territory, and Fairbanks, Alaska. The latter two bases plus others used on the route were set in the midst of a vast wilderness whose surface, heavily wooded, provided relatively few recognisable landmarks for the pilot flying contact. Even in summer a forced landing in the area was hazardous. The hard northern winter furnished distinctive hardships and dangers. The blanket of snow tended to blot out what visual signposts man or nature had provided for the harassed airman. Temperatures often fell below minus 50°F and even passed the minus 70° mark in the record-breaking winter of 1942/43. This altered the characteristic properties of such common materials as rubber, antifreeze solutions, even metal, and of course all lubricants. Ungloved hands froze in a matter of minutes, and contact of flesh with metal was painful. In the bitter cold, sustained activity outdoors was impossible, yet much of the work operating a transport airline for the delivery of aircraft had to be done outdoors. Radio aids to navigation, as they became available, helped, but the Aurora Borealis and related natural phenomena often so distorted signals as to make them unintelligible.

It was the latter months of 1944 which saw not only the peak of the ALSIB ferrying but also the highest level of the Alaskan Division's transport operations in which the C-47 Skytrain played a prominent role. Total ton-miles flown by contract carrier and military crews for the division rose gradually from 1,070,956 in January 1943, to 3,087,348 in September 1944, though this record figure was only a little higher than those for July, August and October of the same year. The best monthly accomplishment in 1945 was nearly as high – 2,877,180 ton miles in June. On the main air link of the route, Edmonton to Fairbanks, which handled about as much traffic as all the other transport lines of the Alaskan Division put together, the major burden was carried from beginning to end by DC-3 transports. Only in August 1945, as hostilities came to an end, were the US contract airlines and their DC-3s withdrawn entirely from the routes of the Alaskan Division.

Early model of the Douglas RD4 transport from VR-4 Squadron
Naval Air Transport Service (NATS), seen over the rugged terrain of
the Aleutians. Navigation aids were few and far between and the
weather was not always as clear as the photograph tends to illustrate.
Snow remained on the high peaks throughout the year. The Alaska-
Aleutians flying operation provided a challenge that put the aircraft to
supreme tests. Crews learned how to winterise the rugged transports
for adaption to the sometimes 40 to 50 degrees below zero
temperatures. The Douglas transport came through with flying
colours. *(Douglas)*

LEFT:
Postwar the C-47 Skytrain continued to serve the USAAF in large numbers including in Alaska where it was often necessary to fit skis for winter operations. Depicted is C-47D-35-DK 44-77152 c/n 33484 showing its skis. This Skytrain also carries the post-war introduced Buzz number on the fuselage – CE-152. It was completed at Oklahoma City in June 1945 and seen somewhere in Alaska in 1947. *(Coombs)*

BELOW:
It was as early as 1940 that the defence of Alaska came under the scrutiny of the US War Department. It was deemed necessary that rapid enforcement by air was apparent from the lessons learnt in Europe. This resulted in an agreement with the Canadian government whereby gold-mining airstrips would be vastly improved from Edmonton to Whitehorse in the Yukon. Depicted parked at Whitehorse is C-47A-90-DL 43-15732 c/n 20198 belonging to the Alaskan Division of the huge US Air Transport Command. Its fin and rudder are painted red as are the outer wings, this aiding rescue in snow covered terrain. *(AP Publications)*

The Alaska Wing of the huge US Air Transport Command was formed on 17 October 1942. There was always a possibility of a Japanese attack on Alaska via the nearby Aleutian chain. The importance of Alaska in World War 2 was further increased when Lend-Lease deliveries to the USSR commenced in August 1942. Troop carrier squadrons of C-47 Skytrains carried 7,500 tons of cargo and 15,000 men per month on intra-theatre flights, mainly to Attu, Adak and Shemya in the Aleutians. Depicted parked in typical frozen north terrain is a C-47A-25-DK Skytrain 42-93600 c/n 13530 of the Alaska Wing ATC with its crew keeping an eye on the team of huskies. *(Douglas)*

Depicted parked at Elmendorf Field, Alaska on 22 February 1945 is C-47C-10-DK 42-108868 c/n 12528, delivered on 27 May 1944 and flown to Alaska for air-sea-rescue duties on 17 November 1944. If too much weight was placed aft, the amphibian had a tendency to tip backwards. The US Army Air Force bought 150 sets of Edo 28 floats but very few Skytrains were converted to amphibious configuration and very little information is available on the use of the C-47C in either Alaska or the Southwest Pacific theatre of operations. *(Duan B. Aceson)*

This C-47 Skytrain from the USAF, shown elevated on a mound of ice above Ice Station Bravo made a forced landing on the ice island in the mid-1950s. The transport was cannibalized leaving only the shell on the wind-eroded mound of ice. Ice Station Bravo, also known as 'T for Tango 3' is located ninety-five miles north of Point Barrow, Alaska, and from 1952 until late 1961, was in use as a USAF weather station and scientific outpost. The unit had to be disbanded and abandoned during late September 1961, when the 2,500 ft runway and eventually the ice-cap, began to break-up and drift away. The C-47 guardian of the island sank to the bottom of the ocean. Shown in the foreground is Captain Glenn Fullencamp USAF, the last Commanding Officer of Ice Station Bravo. *(USAF)*

After VJ-Day in 1945 the task of the RAF transport squadrons in Air Command South-East Asia (ACSEA) was to bring back home the many PoW's which included civilian personnel. Photo depicts a No. 194 'Friendly Firm' Squadron Dakota, one of many, and its load of passengers, whose facial expressions speak for themselves.
(AP Publications)

China – Burma – India and SEAC – ACSEA

The US Ferry Command was renamed Air Transport Command on 20 June 1942. On 6 May 1942 the US War Department had taken over many of the civil airlines' DC-3 transports leaving only 200 to carry on domestic services.

As the situation in China deteriorated, twenty-five DC-3s were transferred to open a supply route across the Himalayas to China. This was the American Military Mission to China known as AMMISCA project. In the event the civil aircraft were considered under-powered, and all but seven C-48s powered by R-1830 engines were re-assigned within the USA and replaced by fifteen C-53 Skytroopers plus at least eight new C-47 Skytrains. Crewed by USAAF reserve officers they formed the 1st Ferry Group of the US 10th Air Force, India and twenty-six aircraft departed the USA for Karachi during April/May 1942. In India the Trans-India Ferry Command and the Assam-Burma-China Ferry Command were formed with four DC-3s and ten borrowed from Pan American Africa and commenced carrying fuel for the raid on Tokyo by Gen Doolittle. They were then diverted to assist Gen Stilwell in northern Burma. A crisis in the Middle East led to the diversion from the theatre of twelve transports from the 10th Air Force.

Late in 1942 the 1st Ferry Group moved from Karachi to Assam. By mid-December fifteen of the sixty-two DC-3s sent to India had been destroyed and four were still in the Middle East. Many others were serviceable, and the airfields in Assam were in a poor state. On 1 December 1942 ATC took over the 'Hump' operation and began to replace the C-47s by the C-46. Despite this eighty-five C-47s were in use before the first Commando arrived, and 160 Skytrains remained in the China-Burma-India theatre even in 1945. The 'Hump' operation by ATC was probably the most important and well-known transport operation in the CBI theatre.

Of the twelve C-47s/C-53s loaned to the Middle East in June 1942 only eight returned and these were kept airworthy by fitting R-1830-47 engines intended for Chinese P-43 Lancer fighters. By the spring of 1943 the 10th Air Force had two C-47 squadrons, the 1st and 2nd Troop Carrier, although the latter was nominally a 14th Air Force unit operating in India. Additionally a third, possibly the 27th Troop Carrier Squadron, was provided for use by Gen Stilwell in Burma. By December 1943, when the joint British-US Eastern Air Command was established, troop carrier command in the 10th Air Force comprised four C-47 units, the 1st., 2nd, 27th and 315th TC squadrons.

The first major tactical use of the troop carrier element was in Orde Wingate's counter attack west of Imphal, Burma on 5 March 1944 during 'Operation Thursday' when a task force comprising thirteen C-47s from the 27th TC Sq., twelve UC-64 Norseman and 150 Waco CG-4A gliders was assembled. Sixty-seven gliders were despatched on what turned out to be an unsatisfactory mission. Only thirty-two reached the landing strip at 'Broadway' where three landed safely, nine landed in Japanese territory, two were lost and the remaining eighteen returned to base. The next day twelve gliders were sent to the landing strip at 'Chowringhee' and between 13/19 March C-47s from the 27th TC Sq flew 156 sorties and dropped over 800,000 lb of supplies. Aerial supply for Wingate and his force continued and the 27th was joined by the 315th TC Sq and No.117 Squadron RAF. While the Wingate expedition was in progress the Japanese were attacking at Imphal resulting in troop carrier command being swamped with requests for help. The 64th Troop Carrier Group consisting of the 4th, 16th, 17th and 35th squadrons arrived on 8 April along with No.216 Squadron RAF, both on emergency detachment from the Middle East to assist in the relief of Imphal.

VVIP Dakota

'A' Flight, the Viceroy's Comm Flight, BAFSEA Comm Squadron, Willingdon, New Delhi (Delhi Race Course) 1942-1946.

'Not only was Dakota KG507 fitted out with an office for use by the Viceroy, Lord Wavell, which included a large desk and swivel chair, and luxury sleeping quarters which included a large double bed. The aircraft had deep pile carpets and a galley which included a refrigerator. Extra radio equipment and a long range fuel tank was fitted. All of this extra equipment and fittings left room for only six passengers and made the aircraft extremely heavy and at times difficult to handle, and quite unlike a normal Dakota.

'The fleet of Dakota transports maintained for the Viceroy and his staff were kept extremely well polished. The Squadron CO paid out of his own pocket to buy metal polish and dusters for the unit's local Indian workforce to polish every inch of the aircraft whenever it was parked at Willingdon. The constant polishing of KG507's airframe by enthusiastic Indian base workers lead to unexpected problems when on an airframe inspection it was found a number of rivet heads had been polished clean off.'

John Williams (RAF pilot)
as told to R.J. Wharton

Java Airlift 1946

Bandoeng air lift is vital supply line, May 1946.

South-east of Batavia, separated from the capital city by 130 miles of narrow roads – roads which have cost lives in all but the most strongly armed convoys and which twist and wind through paddy fields and over steep mountains – lies the city of Bandoeng. Despite continuous patrolling by Allied Forces, extremists infiltrate at night to blow up sections of the road, to lay mines and to fell trees which serve as effective road blocks and mean death from ambushes to the delayed convoys. This treacherous highway is the lifeline of the many civilian and military forces in Bandoeng. To relieve the heavy burden of the too numerous road convoys on this route, No.31 Squadron Transport Command started the Air Supply of Bandoeng. In the peak month of February, when many convoys came under heavy attack, Dakota aircraft of this squadron flew in more than 15 tons of supplies a day, including food, clothing, medical supplies, petrol and ammunition for both the civil and military population.

Today, eight machines of No.31 Squadron, started at dawn on a daily shuttle service, to bring 100 tons of supplies into Bandoeng from Batavia. Sixty per cent of this tonnage goes to feed the population through the Allied Military Administration Civil Affairs Bureau who remove the supplies from the aircraft and check them into store depots. In Bandoeng, emergency food shops have been opened and here civilians can buy essential foods on a ration basis – thanks to these twin-engined aircraft and their crews who daily operate the Bandoeng Airlift.

First in the Indian Skies
Norman L.R. Franks

LEFT:
Dakota 'Peter Oboe' of No.31 Squadron seen parked at Kemajoran in Batavia during the Bandoeng Airlift. With engines running the pilot Flight Lieutenant White is seen in the cockpit, while the navigator (on the left) and Warrant Officer Barnes, pose under the nose of the Dakota. *(IWM)*

BELOW:
The C-47 Skytrain was a workhorse found in all World War 2 theatres of operations. Depicted is C-47A-80-DL 43-15380 c/n 19846 which was assigned to the 14th Air Force in Karachi on 6 May 1944 later being based in China. Earlier in April Gen. Stilwell had launched an attack from Ledo towards Myitkyina using troops of the 50th Chinese Division flown in by C-47 transports of the India-China Wing of Air Transport Command. They were carried forward by the 1st Troop Carrier Squadron to Burma. Vital fuel is being loaded into the C-47 by US personnel watched by Chinese coolies. *(IWM)*

Impressive and quite dramatic photo taken from C-47A-90-DL 43-15696 c/n 20162 belonging to No.1 Air Commando showing its Waco CG-4A Hadrian glider on tow to an advanced airstrip in Burma. Hadrian gliders carried vital airstrip construction equipment and were the first to land on designated sites behind the Japanese lines. The radio link cable between tug and glider can be seen giving a very unusual appearance along the tow-rope. *(AP Publications)*

ABOVE:
The technique of glider-snatch at night was developed successfully by pilots from No.1 Air Commando and commenced operationally on Sunday 5 March 1944 during 'Operation Thursday' when 80 CG-4A gliders with their C-47 tugs took off from Lalaghat, Assam for a night landing behind the Japanese lines. Photo depicts a C-47 Skytrain making a snatch of a Waco CG-4A Hadrian glider in daylight. The system was used by the RAF to retrieve gliders discarded by combat troops which were needed for future airborne operations. *(RAF Museum)*

ABOVE:
Busy World War 2 scene at Kunming, China, with a RAF Dakota on
final approach to land whilst a USAAF C-46 Commando waits its
turn to take-off. Chinese labourers were employed to keep the vital
airfield in working order. Possibly the most important and dangerous
transport operation in the China-India-Burma theatre were the flights
across the Hump from India to China. The US 14th Air Force was
activated and based at Kumning with effect from 10 March 1943. The
weather over the Himalayas was often atrocious and involved flying
on instruments from take-off to landing. *(IWM)*

RIGHT:
RAF Dakota 'Bertie Zebra' from an Air Command South-East Asia
(ACSEA) squadron is parked by the ground crew after another sortie.
One famous Dakota unit was 31 Squadron which helped to break
many records in the theatre. In March 1944 the squadron flew 828
hours by day, 521 at night plus an additional 828 day hours on other
operational duties. In April it dropped 1,471,000 lb of supplies,
transported 427,000 lb and 983 personnel, 103 mules, three horses,
four bullocks, two Bofors guns, one jeep and one motorcycle.
(Chaz Bowyer)

LEFT:
Douglas C-47-DL 41-18548 c/n 4673 seen parked at Barrackpore, India during World War 2. Large serial digits '548' on the fin and rudder and showing the insignia of the huge US Air Transport Command on the fuselage. Completed at Long Beach on 30 August 1942, it was assigned to the US 10th Air Force in India on 23 February 1943 and to the India China Wing of the ATC on 29 May 1943. After returning to the 10th Air Force in Karachi it went to the Government of India on 19 April 1946. *(Peter M. Bowers)*

BELOW:
The 1st Air Commando Group was activated in India on 29 March 1944 commencing operations immediately, being organised to provide fighter cover, bombardment striking power, and air transport services for Wingate's Raiders, the Chindits, who were operating behind Japanese lines under Gen Orde Wingate. The group was unique in being equipped with B-25 Mitchells, P-51 Mustangs, L-1 Vigilants, L-5 Sentinels, R4- Hoverfly helicopters, C-47 Skytrains, CG-4A and TGG-5 gliders and UC-64 Norseman light-cargo transports. First base was Hailakandi, India under Col. Philip G. Cochran. Depicted is an airfield conference with Cochran in the centre of the group whilst in the background is one of the thirteen C-47 transports used by the unit. *(AP Publications)*

Depicted is a RAF Dakota somewhere in Burma with personnel loading auxiliary fuel tanks, possibly for use on Hurricane fighter-bombers. The windows have apertures which could be used for rifles, but not often used. Dakota transports from No.31 Squadron carried Vickers 'K' gas operated machine-guns mounted on pivot supports and protruding through the window frame aft of the wings, port and starboard, the Perspex window having been removed. The photo was taken during July 1944. *(IWM)*

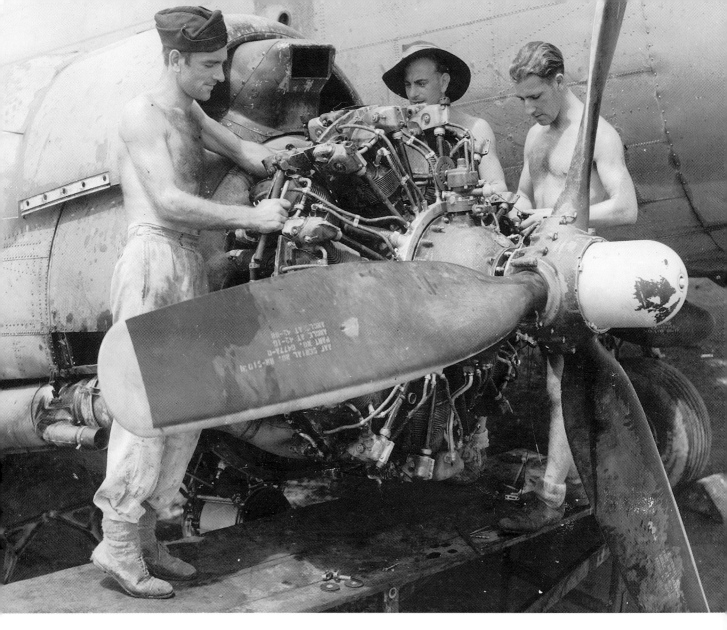

ABOVE:
The versatile Pratt & Whitney R-1830 series of Twin Wasp fourteen cylinder radial engine supported the venerable Douglas transport with its many variants used by the Allies during World War 2 and after. This photo taken in Air Command South-East Asia – ACSEA – shows RAF fitters servicing a Dakota power plant in the field. In the US this engine was built in large numbers under licence by large motor manufacturers such as Buick, whilst in Sweden, a neutral country, a metric version was manufactured by Volvo. The C-47 B were intended for high-altitude operations having 1,200 hp R-1830-90C engines fitted with two-stage blowers. Many had the blowers removed becoming C-47D. *(AP Publications)*

LEFT:
The first major tactical use of the troop carrier element of Allied forces was Gen Orde Wingate's counter attack west of Imphal, Burma in 'Operation Thursday' on 5 March 1944. Between 13 and 19 March C-47 Skytrains of the 27th Troop Carrier Squadron flew 156 sorties and dropped over 800,000 lb of supplies. For clandestine operations behind the Japanese lines Wingate used the mule. These had to be flown into the air strips located at 'Broadway' 'White City' and 'Blackpool'. The recalcitrant Missouri mule required a great deal of persuasion to board the C-47 transport as seen in this photo. *(IWM)*

Douglas Dakotas from RAF Lend-Lease batches were diverted for use by BOAC who operated no less than 60 during and shortly after World War 2. Depicted is G-AGGB in full wartime camouflage and country identification, it being FD773 c/n 6227, and operated in military role when required with the crew wearing RAF uniforms. Ex C-47-DL 42-5639 it was delivered on 13 January 1943 going to BOAC on 19 February and allocated radio call-sign 'ODZAK'. After serving in South Africa and Israel it was withdrawn from use on 30 July 1971 and used for fire practice exercises at Lod Airport, Israel. *(AP Publications)*

Early postwar photo of BOAC Dakota G-AGKN c/n 26429 ex RAF KJ990 radio call-sign 'OFZL' delivered 29 October 1944. It crashed on 14 July 1948 at Cap Sicie near Toulon, France. *(AP Publications)*

B.O.A.C.

Early in 1941 the Government's attention was drawn to the sad state of the British Overseas Airways Corporation aircraft fleet. This consisted of a motley collection of pre-war British and US aircraft inherited from Imperial Airways, plus five DC-3-G102s from KLM which escaped along with their crews when Holland was overrun during May 1940.

At this time everything was being concentrated on the war effort, so, except for three Boeing 314 flying boats, acquired from Pan American Airways, BOAC soldiered on for another year. On 17 December 1942, a British Member of Parliament, Mr W.D. Perkins, again drew the House of Commons attention to the plight of BOAC and the inability of its fleet to keep up the demands made of it. This time the Government acted and through the Lend-Lease scheme, BOAC acquired, together with other aircraft, a number of Douglas Long Beach built C-47-DL Dakota Mk.Is which were delivered between February and April 1943. Fitted with strengthened floors, large double freight doors, and bench seats for twenty-seven passengers along the cabin sides, the first six aircraft, which were powered by two 1,200 hp Pratt & Whitney GR-1830-S1C3-G engines, were delivered with military serials, acquiring civil markings on registration.

By the end of hostilities in Europe, on 8 May 1945, of the fifty-nine Dakotas BOAC had acquired, no fewer than fifty-five survived the war – an excellent record gained under arduous conditions. The unlucky four were – G-AGFZ which overshot the runway at Bromma Airport, Stockholm on 21 April 1944; G-AGIR which crashed into the base of the Atlas mountains SSW of Casablanca at Telmest on 28 August 1944. Captain L.J. White, three passengers and three crew members were killed; G-AGKM had its undercarriage collapse during take-off from El Adem on 8 April 1945. It was operating as KJ992 'OFZM'; G-AGNA crashed at Basra on 1 May 1945.

During the first few months of peace BOAC services continued to expand. The United Kingdom to West Africa and the West Africa to Cairo services were combined. During May daylight flights from Leuchars to Stockholm commenced. On 3 June 1945 Dakota G-AGMZ operated the first twice-weekly Hurn to Karachi service via Istres, Malta, El Adem, Cairo, Baghdad and Sharjah. Lydda and Basra were added on eastbound flights as from early July. Operations located at Leuchars, moved to Croydon on 5 June. KLM operated the Hurn to Gibraltar service under charter, and as from 5 December this was operated by Dakotas of BOAC.

The Dakotas of BOAC were now operating on a civil basis, but mention must be made of two further operations with military significance, in which BOAC with Dakotas took part. In 1947 during *Operation Pakistan*, BOAC and three British independent companies carried 7,000 people from Delhi to Karachi, and about 1,500 in the reverse direction. Food, medicine and vaccine were flown to Delhi and Lahore, BOAC operating twelve Dakotas including G-AGFY, G-AGGB and G-AGHE, alongside their two Avro Yorks and one Avro Lancastrian. The operation commenced on the first day of September and ceased fourteen days later and was under the direction of Air Cdre H.G. Brackley. During the Berlin Airlift in 1948 BOAC operated three Dakotas – G-AGIZ, G-AGNG and G-AGNK – alongside other civil and military operators from 20 October to 25 November. The aircraft, based at Hamburg, carried out eighty-one sorties, flew 224 hours and airlifted 294 tons.

The ubiquitous Dakota was just one of the many aircraft types operated by BOAC during World War 2 and the years that followed. The crews came from far and wide, merchant airmen who did their task without fuss or publicity. It is impossible to be pessimistic of a merchant service which is manned by such as these. They served us well.

Arthur Pearcy Jr – *The Dakota* (1972)

With a D-Day striped C-47 Skytrain transport parked in the background, US Army engineers lay down a metal strip runway shortly after D-Day in June 1944 somewhere in France. The steel matting was known as Pierced Steel Planking (PSP) or Somerfield Tracking, this giving a long period of hard wear and tear. It was necessary to get transports as near to the battle front as possible in order to get vital supplies and ammunition in, and get the casualties out and flown back to the United Kingdom to hospital. *(RAF Museum)*

BELOW:
Once established in Europe the Allies discovered that many of the airfields occupied needed rebuilding after enemy damage etc. Tons of pierced steel planking (PSP) was flown in by Dakotas as seen here with FZ592 c/n 12147 coded 'UZ – Uncle Zulu' from 48 Squadron being unloaded by locally recruited labour. This transport survived World War 2 being sold to Brazil and as PT-KVT crashed on 13 November 1979 some 5 km north of Cascavel, Parana. *(IWM)*

US 9th Troop Carrier Command

Reactivation of the US 9th Air Force took place in the United Kingdom on 16 October 1943. The original cadre came from the headquarters of 1st Troop Carrier Command and the new 9th Troop Carrier Command was activated under the command of Brigadier-General Benjamin F. Giles. Under it was placed the 50th Troop Carrier Wing under the command of Brigadier-General Julian M. Chappel. The headquarters element of the Wing had just arrived from the USA and was composed of personnel with three years of troop carrier operations behind them. Assigned to the Wing were the 315th Troop Carrier Group under Colonel Hamish McLelland and with two squadrons only – the 34th and 43rd. These had been in the theatre with the US 8th Air Force since December 1942. They were joined by the complete 434th Troop Carrier Group under Lt-Col Fred D. Stevers having just arrived in the UK from the USA.

The first 9th Troop Carrier Command was initially based at Cottesmore, Rutland but moved to Grantham, Lincolnshire on 1 December 1943. The 50th Wing was at Cottesmore then moved to Bottesford, Leicestershire on 18 November 1943. The 315th Troop Carrier Group moved from Aldermaston, Berkshire to Welford also in Berkshire on 6 November 1943 and to Spanhoe, Northamptonshire on 7 February 1944. The 434th Troop Carrier Group was at Fulbeck, Lincolnshire until 10 December 1943 when it moved to Welford Park, Berkshire. On 3 November 1943 the 435th Troop Carrier Group under the command of Colonel Frank J. MacNees arrived at Langar, Nottinghamshire assigned to the 50th Wing moving to Welford Park on 25 January 1944.

All fifteen groups of the 9th Troop Carrier Command were to take part in the opening move of the invasion. Their transports were to deliver paratroops and glider-borne infantry of the US 82nd and 101st Airborne Divisions on six drop or landing zones in close proximity to St. Mere Eglise. From there the troops would seize bridges, roads and other key points to assist the inland progress of the troops landed on Utah Beach. First dispatched were six Pathfinder serials – three aircraft to each serial except one which had four. Their task was to drop Pathfinder teams in each of the drop zones (DZ), these teams would mark each landing zone for the remainder of the troops. All six drops were accomplished.

While the Pathfinders were operating, 821 C-47 Skytrains and C-53 Skytroopers plus another 104 transports towing Waco CG-4A gliders were ready to be dispatched in twenty-eight serials from fourteen airfields from Lincolnshire to Devon. The first serials took off from Greenham Common, these being the C-47s of the 438th TCGrp taking off at eleven second intervals. The leader of the first serial was the CO of the 438th Colonel John Donaldson flying *Birmingham Belle*. The aircraft was airborne at 2248 hours on 5 June 1944.

The paratroops were resupplied between 2053 and 2250 hours in the early evening of 6 June, and between 0700 and 0855 on 7 June by 408 tugs towing 408 Waco CG-4A gliders in nine serials. Waco gliders were used for night landings and the heavier Horsa for when there was daylight. Further resupply was carried out on the morning of 7 June by 320 C-47s and C-53s. All things considered the airborne operations through to the morning of 7 June, when the last sortie was flown, were a success. In total 1,662 transports and 512 gliders were dispatched. Some 1,606 transports and 512 gliders crossed the English Channel and 1,581 aircraft completed their mission while 503 gliders were released on their landing zone. Forty-one troop carrier aircraft were lost and 449 suffered damage.

Seen on return to base at Juvincourt, France are thirty Skytrains from the 439th Troop Carrier Group 91st Squadron after dropping paratroops at Groesbeek, Holland on 17 September 1944. 1/Lt Donald G. LePard is flying C-47A-75-DL 42-100847 c/n 19308 L4 – B for Bertie. Photo taken by the Group Commander, Lt/Col Charles H. Young flying *The Argonia* 43-15159 c/n 19625 from the 94th Squadron code 'D8'. *(Colonel Charles H. Young)*

ABOVE:

The Rhine crossing in March 1945 was the final and largest airborne assault of World War 2 with some 1,500 troop carriers and gliders taking part. Seen parked at Coulommiers/Voisins, France on 24 March 1945 are Skytrain tugs from the 437th Troop Carrier Group, 83rd Squadron in the foreground – code 'T2'. The Waco CG-4A gliders carried the US 17th Airborne Division with each Douglas transport towing two gliders, releasing them near Wesel on the Rhine. *(IWM)*

LEFT:

By 18 January 1945, the Battle of Bastogne was over, won by the stubborn troopers of the US 101st Airborne Division. The Mayor of Bastogne presented them with the flag of the town which was accepted on behalf of the US troops. Fuel for tanks, armoured vehicles etc was a vital necessity during the battle so C-47 Skytrains based in France flew in gasoline as depicted in this photo of C-47A-75-DL 'H for Harry' with its precious cargo being unloaded. This transport 42-100938 c/n 19401 was salvaged after an accident on 26 June 1944, was repaired and put back into service. *(IWM)*

ABOVE:
The huge US 9th Troop Carrier Command, initially based in the
United Kingdom, used the Waco CG-4A glider for night operations,
and the heavier British built Airspeed Horsa in daylight. Depicted
taking off from Greenham Common, Berkshire, is Long Beach built
C-47A-70-DL 42-100770 coded 4U – H for Harry from the 89th
Troop Carrier Squadron, 438th Troop Carrier Group, 53rd Troop
Carrier Wing, towing a Horsa glider. This C-47 was reported missing
in action over Europe on 16 October 1944. *(IWM)*

RIGHT:
'Operation Market' was the air landings of the US 82nd Airborne
Division near Nijmegen and the US 101st Airborne Division, north of
Eindhoven, Holland, fifty miles behind enemy lines in a daylight
operation. Naturally there were aircraft casualties as depicted by the
photo of the remains of a USAAF C-47 Skytrain. *(IWM)*

LEFT:
'Operation Repulse' was the relief of US forces encircled by the Germans at Bastogne on 20 December, 1944. A supply drop by 116 C-47 Skytrains on Christmas Day had to be cancelled due to weather. Supplies of ammunition was low and ten Waco gliders were loaded with sixteen tons, mainly ammunition, and were towed off from Orleans, France by the 440th Troop Carrier Group, for the 265-mile flight to Bastogne. There were both tug and glider casualties. Depicted is the remains of a C-47A-75-DL G for George from a squadron from the 440th TC Group which was reported missing in action on 29 December, 1944. It is 42-100904. *(IWM)*

BELOW:
A very long line of USAAF C-47 Skytrains from the 9th Troop Carrier Command are seen in line on an airfield in France awaiting instructions to fly supplies including vital vehicle fuel to the US 3rd Army cut-off in the Battle of the Bulge in December 1944. The first few aircraft carry the nose code '6Z' belonging to the 96th Squadron 440th Troop Carrier Group based at Orleans, France. The group returned to the USA on 3 September 1947 after receiving a Distinguished Unit Citation for its efforts on 6/7 June 1944. *(IWM)*

Four Douglas C-47 Skytrain transports from the 442nd Troop Transport Group, 305th Squadron seen in formation over Europe. The first transport is a C-47A-80-DL 43-15126 c/n 19592 4J – H for Harry which survived World War 2 and sold in Sweden, later going to a French airline and crashed at Luang Prabang in Indo China on 12 February 1951. After USAAF service in Europe it was disposed of by the US Foreign Liquidation Commission. *(Darrel Warner)*

ABOVE:
Douglas C-47-DL 41-18376 c/n 4414 named *Miss Carriage* seen from another transport flying low level over the ocean. It was one of the early USAAF arrivals in the United Kingdom during 1942 assigned to the US Eighth Air Force. Forward planning called for a build-up of fifteen Troop Carrier Groups in the UK by the end of 1943. During August 1942 however came 'Operation Torch' the invasion of North Africa so three transport groups were transferred to the US 12th Air Force. Serving in Italy the C-47 survived World War 2 going to the Foreign Liquidation Commission (FLC) on 11 December 1945 and is reputedly still in commercial service in Colombia today. *(IWM)*

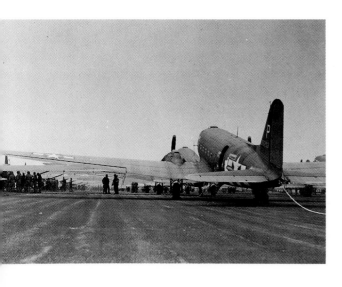

LEFT:
The huge US 9th Troop Carrier Command, with its three Troop Carrier Wings – 50th, 52nd and 53rd – operated a total of 15 Troop Carrier Groups, each with four squadrons of C-47 Skytrains with thirteen in each squadron. By 6 June 1944 these were all occupying over 15 airfields. Depicted is a typical USAAF base scene as two lines of C-47s are positioned on the runway whilst a line of Waco CG-4A gliders are parked at each side on the grass. The Skytrain near the camera is 43-15203 c/n 19669 'P for Peter' from an unidentified troop carrier squadron. *(AP Publications)*

71

RIGHT:
Many months of rehearsals were completed prior to Operation Overlord, the D-Day landings 6 June 1944. During these rehearsals it was inevitable that with such a large airborne force involved there was air and ground accidents. Depicted at Cottesmore, Rutland, base for the 316th Troop Carrier Squadron with its four squadrons, is a Skytrain from the 36th Squadron – code '6E' after a ground collision just prior to D-Day. The pilot was unfortunately killed. *(AP Publications)*

OPPOSITE TOP:
Seen engaged in paratroop training exercises with the Allies at Camp d'Avord, France, is veteran C-47A-65-DL 42-100533 '7D – B for Bertie' from the 80th Troop Carrier Squadron, 436th Troop Carrier Group based at Melun Villaroche, France. Its many combat missions are recorded on the front fuselage panel. It survived World War 2 serving in Germany with effect from 1 January 1948 and was finally reclaimed at Burtonwood here in the United Kingdom on 31 May 1950. *(Silvestre Collection)*

BELOW:
With the end of hostilities in Europe, an element of the huge US 9th Troop Carrier Command was retained as part of the new United States Air Forces in Europe. This included men and planes from the 442nd Troop Carrier Group which had arrived from the USA in March 1944 being based initially at Fulbeck, Lincolnshire then Weston Zoyland, Somerset. Depicted C-47A-10-DK 42-92877 c/n 12726 4J – B for Bertie from the 305th Squadron seen parked on the huge apron at Tempelhof, Berlin. It still carries the tote of sorties carried out on the fuselage. *(Darrel Warner)*

LEFT:
Nose art on C-47 Skytrains was never prolific as that portrayed on the USAAF bombers and fighters. Depicted is C-47B-15-DK 43-49358 c/n 26619 *Leading Lady* from the 4th Troop Carrier Squadron, 62nd Troop Carrier Group, which was activated at McClellan in California on 11 December 1940. It moved to the United Kingdom in August/September 1942, taking part in the North African campaign in Tunisia after moving to Tafaroui, Algeria in November. It remained with the US 12th Air Force and served with great distinction in the Mediterranean theatre of operations. The pilot was Lt W.H. Lynn and Engineer Sgt. E.A. Croffold. *(AP Publications)*

The first transport to land on a hurriedly prepared steel mesh airfield in France after D-Day was this Douglas C-47 Skytrain, bringing in vital supplies including ammunition for the airborne forces, taking out casualties on its return flight to the United Kingdom. Suitably marked oil drums mark the side of the runway. Pierced steel planking – PSP – was also used for temporary runways in operational theatres. *(Douglas)*

US paratroops seen boarding a Red Cross marked C-53 Skytrooper of the 63rd Transport Group which in 1940 was based at Wright Field, Ohio, and utilising the C-33, C-34 (DC-2) and C-50 (DC-3) later converting to the C-47 Skytrain and C-53. This Skytrooper could be 41-20086 c/n 4856 delivered in 1942 when the unit was based at Camp Williams, Wisconsin. During World War 2 this group transported supplies, material and personnel in the US and the Caribbean area. In April 1942 it became part of the huge US Air Transport Command. *(Via Jerry Scutts)*

Appropriately registered NC41HQ and finished in US Army Air Corps livery a very rare DC-3 type visited the UK for the 50th Anniversary of D-Day celebrations in 1994. The first US Army DC-3, the C-41 (DC-3-253) 38-502 c/n 2053 was an off-the-shelf DC-3A delivered for use by General 'Hap' Arnold on 11 October 1938. Its interior was configured as a 14-seat luxury passenger military executive transport. During World War 2 it accumulated 2,739 hours. On 16 April 1945 it was acquired by Alaska Airlines and three years later went to the CAA as an airways flight check transport, registered NC12 then N43. Its current owner, Otis Spunkmeyer, acquired the C-41 on 1 March 1989. Aircraft is seen parked at Wroughton on 9 June 1994. *(Peter R. Arnold)*

Casualty Evacuation

Throughout the months of 1943 there had been much argument and discussion over the arrangements for the evacuation of casualties, and it was not until 22 May 1944 that a definite policy was agreed upon. A casualty rate of 600 per day by D-Day +40 was allowed for and these were to be accepted at 200 per day at centres adjacent the airfields located at RAF Broadwell, Blakehill Farm and Down Ampney, all bases for RAF Dakota squadrons. No.46 Group completed its first task of casualty evacuation one week after D-Day when Dakotas flew 23 Army and one RAF casualty from France to RAF Blakehill Farm. By 28 July 1944, 10,000 casualties had been transported back to the UK.

By the end of November 1944, over 47,000 sick and wounded from the Western Front in Europe, had been flown to hospitals in the UK by aircraft of RAF Transport Command. Every one of them was in the care of the RAF Medical Branch from the time they entered the aircraft, usually a Dakota, on a landing strip in Europe, until they were distributed to Army medical establishments and hospitals in the UK.

The national daily newspapers here in the UK revealed for the first time on Saturday 14 June 1944, eight days after D-Day, that RAF Dakota transports with WAAF nursing orderlies were being used to bring back casualties from the invasion front in France. The first flight, according to the newspapers, was an experiment and the extent to which air evacuation of wounded replacing evacuation by sea largely depended on a verdict by the Air Ministry. The flights to the Continent were approved by the Air Ministry and soon operated on a regular basis.

The first three WAAF nursing orderlies were Corporal Lydia Alford, Leading Aircraft Women (LAC) Myra Roberts and LAC Edna Birbeck. Edna recalls her experiences:

'We were attached to No.233 Squadron based at RAF Blakehill Farm, near Cricklade, joining the unit at the end of March 1944. My first flight in a Dakota was on 20 April which was a training flight for the crew, and the aircraft was without its cargo doors. I was feeling sick so left the cabin for the 'little room' at the rear. The Wireless Operator realised I had gone and was terrified, thinking I had fallen out. All was well when I appeared looking slightly green. The W/Op was Glyn 'Taffy' Morris who I eventually married. Another nurse married the navigator from the same 233 Squadron Dakota crew. Both on 31 March 1945.

'Prior to D-Day I did a refresher course at RAF Wroughton hospital. At RAF Blakehill Farm there was a large field hospital – a Casualty Air Evacuation Centre – under canvas, during the early days after the Normandy landings, but later all casualties were moved out by ambulance after arrival by Dakota. Later we landed casualties at CAEC's located at RAF Down Ampney and Broadwell. I personally escorted by air a total of 630 casualties from the war front, including 526 stretcher and 104 sitting cases. The bases flown to in Europe were numerous.

'Our first operational sortie took place on Friday 13 June 1944, and three nurses chosen for the task were confined to Sick Quarters the night before, with only a vague idea of what was happening. At dawn on the day, after an aircrew breakfast, we were taken out to our three Dakotas. The crew of our Dak were Australian – Flg Off Hamilton and W/op Sgt Jimmy Firth who were later killed at Arnhem – we had an escort of Spitfires as we crossed the Channel, and as we approached the French coast the sea appeared to be full of small boats. The landing was on a metal strip runway laid down in a field of corn with poppies still in bloom around the edges, but it was like a sandstorm when the Dakota landed and we were all soon smothered in yellow dust. The aircraft was quickly loaded with wounded – the first evacuation of wounded from France by air had been successfully completed.

By 28 July 1944, over 10,000 casualties had been airlifted back to the United Kingdom from the battleground in Europe. Eight days after D-Day on 14 June 1944 the first RAF Dakota transports with WAAF nursing orderlies on board were bringing back casualties from the invasion front in France. On 18 June casualties were airlifted by Dakota from B4 airstrip Beny Sur Mer, under fire from the enemy. Photo depicts a casualty being inspected by a nursing sister from the Princess Mary RAF Nursing Service whilst WAAF orderlies look on. A control HQ at Swindon, Wiltshire was in direct contact with airfields, hospitals and ambulance units. *(AP Publications)*

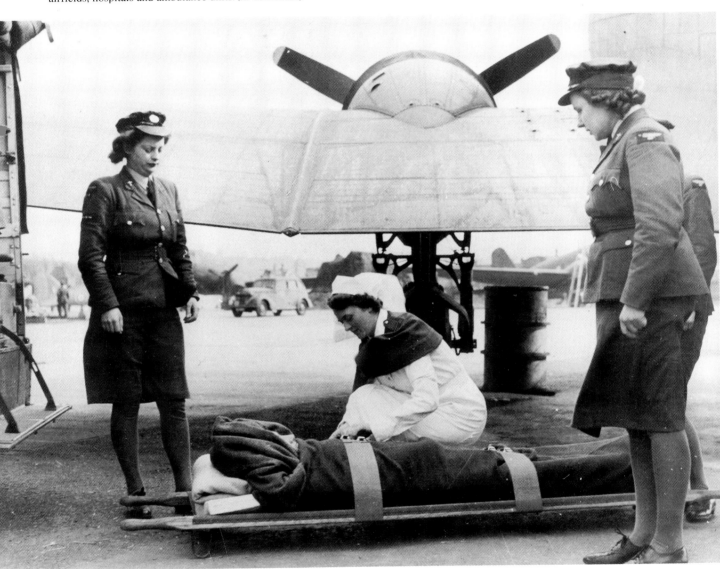

ABOVE:
An early Long Beach built C-47-DL 42-5681 c/n 7375 delivered on 24 January 1943 was equipped as a casualty evacuation (CASEVAC) transport having a capability of carrying up to 24 litter patients. It is depicted at Mitchell Field, New York, during an Open House demonstration to New York high school graduates. Many lives were saved during World War 2 in all theatres of operations, thanks to the Skytrain converted as a carrier for the sick and wounded. *(USAF)*

LEFT:
Skytrain transports equipped as ambulance aircraft seen parked on a newly constructed airstrip in France waiting to take on board wounded personnel to be flown back to hospitals in the United Kingdom. The nearest Skytrain is C-47-DL 41-18528 c/n 4620 which operated in the Western Desert in November 1942, joining the US 9th Troop Carrier Command on 10 August 1944. After an accident it was salvaged on 6 May 1945. *(RAF Museum)*

Dramatic post-war photo depicting a C-47A-80-DL Skytrain 43-15287 c/n 19753 on final approach in preparation to snatch the parked Waco CG-4A Hadrian glider. The trailing hook for pick-up can clearly be seen extended from the transport's fuselage plus the external pick-up winch. Photo taken during August 1949 at Stewart AFB, New York during filming of the movie *Wings Over West Point*. *(Paul Paulson)*

BELOW:
Rare photo depicting a Whitley bomber modified for dropping paratroops, and an early RAF Dakota, both from No.1 Parachute Training School at Ringway, dropping paratroops on the nearby dropping zone at Tatton Park. The Whitley carried ten, the Dakota twenty using the side cargo door for exit, whilst the Whitley dropped from a hole in the fuselage. The Dakota was versatile during airborne operations being used as a glider tug, and for glider pick-up or 'snatch' in addition to normal cargo/troop duties. It was 1943 before the RAF received their first Dakota under Lend-Lease. *(PRB MoD)*

Airborne Forces

By early January 1943 Sir Alan Brooke, Commander-in-Chief, Home Forces, requested that America be asked to supply as many Waco gliders as we needed, and that the provision of transport aircraft be accelerated by all means possible. Throughout 1942/43 requests were continuously being made by the Parachute Training School located at Ringway airport Manchester for the allotment to them of Dakota aircraft, or even an old or crashed fuselage, so that side door jumping experience could be gained by instructors. The experience of the 1st Parachute Brigade in North Africa during November 1942 added weight to the appeal. Then USAAF C-47 Skytrains were used. But the PTS request could not be granted until September 1943. Until then the few Dakotas available were urgently needed for transport work, and the transport pilots did their work so well that not even a crashed fuselage became available.

The Dakota was required in order that the instructional staff might increase their already extensive knowledge and experience of parachute jumping. During the first airborne operation in North Africa on 8 November 1942 involving 39 C-47 Skytrains, 25 of the transports carried newly trained RAF navigators. Back in May 1942 No.4 Middle East Training School came into being at Kabrit, Palestine and on 13 March 1943 it moved to Ramat David. Also during March the US 7th Troop Carrier Squadron arrived to carry out exercises in conjunction with No.4 Parachute Brigade, staying until the end of May bringing with them thirteen C-47 Skytrains.

Operation 'Ladbrooke' against Syracuse, Sicily, took place on the night of 9/10 July and was assisted by 109 C-47 Skytrain transports from USAAF Troop Carrier Command. Unfortunately the US aircrew were unaccustomed to flak, the C-47 was not armoured and had no self-sealing tanks and their navigators were not up to standard. The cost in gliders and men was considerable although none of the 134 C-47 tugs was lost.

With the delivery of the first Lend-Lease Dakotas which equipped squadrons in the Middle East under No.216 Group airborne training commenced. In August 1943 eight RAF Dakotas undertook tactical exercises with No.11 Parachute Battalion at Ramat David, Palestine, the training being completed by 17 October. Earlier on 15 September six Dakotas dropped paratroops on the Greek island of Cos. The drop was completely successful and three days later 14 Dakotas and three Lockheed Hudsons dropped supplies. Four subsequent supply drops took place, two by night, until 25 September when the paratroops were airlifted off the island.

Operation 'Accolade' was planned for September 1943 against the island of Rhodes in the Aegean Sea but was cancelled when it became known that the Germans were in complete control of the island of Rhodes. A successful night operation was carried out on 31 October and the following night when 200 troops of the Greek Sacred Squadron were dropped on Samos. Five Dakotas dropped 100 troops on each night and a sixth Dakota followed up with supplies.

For a long time prior to the invasion of Europe on 6 June 1944 the fact that ultimately it was inevitable, failing an unexpected and almost total collapse of German resistance, was realised, but it could not be said that any really practical planning took place until April 1943 when Lt.-Gen. F.E. Morgan, Chief of Staff to the Supreme Allied Commander was instructed to plan for the invasion of Europe. The plan for operation 'Overlord' was to be prepared and ready by 1 August 1943. The aim of the proposed invasion was to land large forces of British and American troops somewhere on the coast of Europe so as to make the destruction of the German forces in NW Europe strategically possible and eventually to launch an onslaught against Germany itself.

The rest is history and adequately recorded elsewhere.

By 1947 no less than 72 Dakotas were in service with the Royal
Canadian Air Force who assigned numerous varied roles for the
transport. Depicted equipped in the RESCUE role is KG568 c/n
13160 ex 42-93267 which went to the RAF on 8 May 1944, ferried to
the UK by 30 May eventually joining No.437 RCAF Squadron, being
ferried back to Canada after World War 2 service in Europe. On 21
March 1962 it was bought by the Indian Air Force becoming BJ763.
(AP Publications)

Royal Canadian Air Force

The Douglas Dakota first went into regular service with the RCAF on 29 March 1943 when aircraft No.650 c/n 9015 ex 42-32789 was delivered to No.12 Communications Squadron at Rockcliffe. In April it was transferred to No.164 Squadron based at Moncton, New Brunswick. The transport survived World War 2 becoming a ground instruction airframe 'A508' on 12 July 1946, finally being struck off charge on 2 February 1953.

Records reveal that the Royal Canadian Air Force (RCAF) received about 570 Dakotas under the huge Allied Lend-Lease programme during World War 2, the type operating alongside the RAF in various theatres of operations. Two squadrons – 435 and 436 – were formed in India in Air Command South-East Asia (ACSEA) serving in Burma, whilst another squadron – 437 – was formed in the United Kingdom and served in the liberation of Europe. These squadrons flew their aircraft to Canada in 1946 and became part of the peacetime transport element with the RCAF. Later some were employed on vital United Nations relief work in the Middle East, whilst others came back to Europe to support the Canadian forces in NATO.

Many Dakotas operated with the RCAF in their original RAF serial identification, whilst others supplied direct to Canada were given three digit serial numbers in the blocks '650 to 664' and '960 to 964' whilst '1000' was reserved later for a VIP aircraft, and a further nine were purchased during the 1950s with serials '10910 to 10918'. With the formation of the unified Canadian Armed Forces (CAF) in 1968, all Dakotas were given new serial numbers consisting of five digits. The transports '12901 to 12971' were designated CC-129 in 1970 and two '12938' and '12959' were used for electronics training and fitted with a 8-ft nose spike and equipped with radar from the F-104 Starfighter.

Many RCAF Dakotas used during World War 2 were passed back to the RAF or sold to civil operators including a batch in Canada for Trans Canada Airlines. Of the 111 carrying RAF serials post-war 43 survived to be renumbered as mentioned earlier, the balance being made up of those with original RCAF serial numbers. The last 70 odd were sold to either Canadians or operators in the USA with odd ones used for spares. A number were transferred to the Indian Air Force during 1962/63.

The last flight by Canadian Armed Forces Dakotas on 31 March and 1 April 1989 was well attended by veterans and enthusiasts of the type. It was announced that two transports would be retained for preservation in museums, the rest to be sold. On 25 July 1991 six stored CAF Dakotas were sold to the Fleming Corporation of Nashua, New Hampshire and destined for conversion to turboprop configuration by Warren Basler. They received the following registrations: 12907 c/n 27187 N92BF: 12933 c/n 13383 N103BF: 12937 c/n 9415 N400BF: 12938 c/n 9832 N21BF: 12950 c/n 12543 N104BF: 12957 c/n 26002 N92BF.

All the Dakotas were in pristine stock condition and it is most unfortunate they were not allowed to join the ever growing C-47 Dakota or Gooney Bird warbird movement, but at least we hope they will keep flying, albeit in a highly modified form.

RIGHT:
The Dakota has been employed on target-towing duties with both the South African Air Force and the Royal Canadian Air Force. Depicted with black/yellow stripes on the tail and under the wings is RCAF Dakota KG580 c/n 13303 which went to the RAF on 19 May 1944, arriving in the UK on 4 June and eventually serving with RCAF squadrons in Europe before returning to Canada on 16 April 1946. Note the tail guard on the Dakota and the installation as used to tow gliders was used. *(AP Publications)*

BELOW:
Up to 1958 the RAF had navigators trained with the RCAF at 2 Air Observer School equipped with Dakotas. On 1 February 1968 all aircraft were consolidated in a single inventory under the Canadian Armed Forces and the school based at Winnipeg, Manitoba had twenty-two Dakotas on its inventory. This unit received national recognition during 1969 for its superb flight safety record covering five years of accident-free flying, involving over 85,000 hours in the air. Depicted pre 1968 is the flight line from the school at Winnipeg. Note the radar tub under each Dakota fuselage. *(AP Publications)*

The Royal Canadian Air Force (RCAF) received nearly 600 Dakotas during World War 2 under the huge Allied Lend-Lease programme, many of these operating alongside the RAF in various theatres of operations. Two squadrons – 435 and 436 – were formed in Air Command South-East Asia (ACSEA) and served in Burma, whilst 437 Squadron was formed in the United Kingdom and served in Europe. After World War 2 all three squadrons with their Dakotas were flown back to Canada. The last Dakotas of the Canadian Armed Forces – now a unified force – were gracefully retired on 31 March 1989 and put up for disposal. Two of the veterans are depicted.

(AP Publications)

For 46 years the Dakota served Canada's air arm – RCAF later CAF – as a venerable workhorse and were respected and kept in immaculate condition as seen in this impressive photo of CAF Dakota 12963 seen at the Gimli Air Show in 1982. Delivered to the RAF in January 1944 it served with 512 and 48 Squadron prior to going to the RCAF in Europe. Along with others it was retired in March 1989 and is in cold storage today. *(AP Publications)*

LEFT:
Dakotas of the RCAF later CAF were employed as cargo carriers operating in snow and ice covered areas along the Mid-Canada Line, the early warning radar network – DEWLINE – which roughly followed the 55th parallel. The winter of 1946/47 was a very cold one and -82F was recorded at Snag and a RCAF Dakota landed at the Watson Lake airstrip in -50F. Depicted is FZ692 of the CAF using RATOG bottles for assisted take-off. Today the aircraft is a survivor owned by Innotech Aviation Enterprises Inc. *(AP Publications)*

BELOW:
Two RCAF Dakota transports were equipped with the spike-nose which was a Lockheed F-104 Starfighter radome. The cockpit was a complete F-104G mockup, test and measuring equipment permitting in-flight evaluation of the Starfighter's all-weather, advanced radar and fire control equipment. The eight-foot nose spike carried the interchangeable electronics gear, which became standard on hundreds of NATO F-104 fighters. Depicted is *Dolly's Folly* 12938 which along with *Pinocchio* 12959 returned to Cold Lake in 1962 for their nose job. The third Dakota of this type, *Woody Woodpecker* fell victim to a crash. *(AP Publications)*

RIGHT:
With a full load of rice a crew from No.436 Squadron RCAF Dakota
climb over the cargo with the CO Wing Commander R. Gordon DFC
followed by (L to R) F/O G.B. Coyle, F/O F.V. Cooper, F/O C.O.
Simpson and Flt/Lt J.W. Dolphin. Over a period of eight months
No.435/436 Squadron flew 120 hours a day and put 29,783 hours on
the Dakota airframes, consuming about 1,760,000 gallons of fuel and
flying over 4 million miles. A total of 14,400 passengers were carried
and 851 casualties evacuated from the battle area by air. The
squadrons were part of the huge Allied Combat Cargo Task Force in
South-East Asia. *(RCAF)*

BELOW:
Frequent scene at London (Gatwick) Airport with a Royal Canadian
Air Force Dakota '972' from No.1 Air Division based in Europe with
NATO taking on cargo. The Dakota was delivered to the RCAF on 28
July 1944, becoming '10972' in Europe in April 1956, returning to
Canada as '972' and with the unification of the armed forces became
'12955' in June 1970. It was sold as CF-BKT and today is in the
USA as N300ZZ. *(AP Publications)*

The Royal Canadian Air Force contributed three Dakota squadrons, one in Europe and two in Air Command South-East Asia (ACSEA), during World War 2. Depicted is RCAF Dakota KN665 'W for Whisky' seen parked at Mauripur, Northern India on 10 November 1947. It is a C-47B-35-DK 44-77036 c/n 33368 delivered on 26 May 1945 going to the RAF on 9 June, and arriving in the UK on 14 June. It went out to India with No.77 Squadron on 29 August. It joined No.435 Squadron RCAF on 29 September and No.436 on 17 March 1946. This transport is a survivor today being registered N132AL with Michael A. Spisak, Kotzebue, in Alaska. *(Ray Sturtivant)*

The sleek revised lines of the Super DC-3 are very apparent in this view of the prototype Super DC-3 N30000 c/n 43158 taken on 20 July 1949. It was a lengthened fuselage, with doors covering the mainwheels and a semi-retractable tail wheel fitted. It made its maiden flight on 26 June 1949. In 1951 it went to the USAF for flight trials, then to the US Navy where it remained in service as BuNo.138820. On 2 July 1981 it was registered N117LR to Roy D. Reagan of Chico, California and survives today. *(Douglas)*

Super DC-3

After the end of World War 2, a number of DC-3 replacement transports appeared on the market. These were considerably faster, had a greater passenger and cargo capacity and were naturally much more expensive than the DC-3. After rebuilding some war surplus C-47s and C-117s as the DC-3C and DC-3D. Douglas quickly decided to act on the old adage – 'that the only replacement for a DC-3 was another DC-3.'

To save engineering time and cost and to reduce the price whilst providing new life for the large number of DC-3s and derivatives which were threatened by expiry of their airworthiness certificates in 1952, Douglas concentrated his efforts on modernising existing aircraft rather than designing an entirely new transport. After initial design work had been completed by a team comprising many of the DC-3's original designers, the project was transferred to a special group headed by Malcolm K. Oleson a Douglas project engineer. To meet new regulations the aircraft's stability, single-engine performance and take-off had to be improved, plus the speed.

Utilising two second-hand aircraft – an ex C-47-DL 41-18656 c/n 6017 and an ex DC-3 NC15579 c/n 4122 Douglas commenced to build two prototypes of the new DC-3S better known as the Super DC-3. In addition to the fuselage structure being strengthened, a 3ft 3in section with an extra window on each side was added to the fuselage forward of the front wing spar – this increasing the normal seating capacity to 30 – and the passenger door, acting also as an integral airstair, was moved forward.

New vertical and horizontal tail surfaces with squared tips and increased area were fitted and the dorsal fin area was substantially increased to improve single-engine handling. The wing centre section was left unchanged but new outer panels with squared tips and 15.5 degree sweep on the leading edge and a four degree sweep on the trailing edge replacing the original wing outboard sections. Wing span was reduced from 95 ft of the standard DC-3 to 90 ft and the wing area was reduced from its 986 sq ft to 969 sq ft. New engine nacelles with doors enclosing the fully strengthened undercarriage were designed to accommodate a choice of two engines, either the 1,475 hp Wright Cyclone R-1820-C9HE nine-cylinder radials or the 1,450 hp Pratt & Whitney R-2000-D7 fourteen-cylinder radials driving fully-feathering propellers.

After completion of an extensive modernisation, c/n 6017 emerged as the first DC-3S with the new serial c/n 43158 and registered N30000. Powered by Wright Cyclone engines, it made its first flight from Clover Field on 23 June 1949 with John F. Martin at the controls. Flight test results exceeded expectations and there was little doubt that the Super DC-3 would meet all Civil Air Regulation requirements whilst offering an increase in payload and performance.

In spite of offering improved performance, the commercial Super DC-3 sales effort proved a failure and as a result of the US sales tour only Capital Airlines showed an interest in the new airliner, resulting in an order for three Wright R-1820-C9HE powered aircraft. The second prototype was acquired by a construction company. The Capital Airlines aircraft were N16019 c/n 43191: N16016 c/n 43192 and N16016 c/n 43192.

Having failed to sell the Super DC-3 to the airlines, Douglas sold the prototype c/n 43158 to the US Air Force who allocated it the serial 51-3817 designated YC-129 later changed to YC-47F. Following extensive flight trials and heavily modified, the USAF decided not to adopt the YC-47F and the aircraft was transferred to the US Navy who designated it R4D-8X with BuNo. 13820. The result was the US Navy awarded Douglas a contract to modify 100 of their large fleet of R4D-5s, R4D-6s and R4D-7s which became R4D-8 in the new configuration.

The US Naval Arctic Research Laboratory (NARL), located some 330 miles north of the Arctic circle, was established in 1947. Over the years it operated both the R4D- Skytrain and the R4D-8 Super DC-3 transport in its research activities. Depicted is civilian contracted pilot, Dick Delafield standing by Super DC-3 BuNo.12431 registered N31310 c/n 43395 delivered to the NARL at Point Barrow, Alaska on 14 April 1976, serving until 1982. *(L. Makashima)*

Beautifully preserved today in flying condition in Florida by Super Three Inc. of Coral Gables is this immaculate example of C-117D N99857 c/n 43332 who bought the transport on 3 July 1990. Its registration is the same as its US Navy BuNo.99857 although N456WL was originally allocated. Its nautical career included service at Barbers Point, Hawaii, Alameda and North Island in California, and Iwakuni, Japan with the US Marine Corps. It was held in storage at Davis-Monthan, Arizona between April 1971 and October 1981. *(Michael Prophet)*

BELOW:
Excellent profile air to air photo of Super DC-3 'Douglas C-117' C-CDOG c/n 43374 in the livery of Millardair of Toronto. This is one of a handful of Super DC-3s operated by the company but now withdrawn from use. This transport had BuNo.17248 ex c/n 25446 which after service with the US Navy which included European assignments to Naples and Blackbushe, the latter with FASRON-200, went into storage at Davis-Monthan, Arizona in October 1981. The same month it was registered N1334K to TBM Inc. a fire-bomber company. It later went to Canada being withdrawn from use on 31 May 1990. *(Paul Duffy)*

After a busy World War 2 career with squadrons of the Naval Air
Transport Service as an R4D-5, BuNo.50762 c/n 26278 was one of
100 selected for conversion to Super DC-3 standard. It is depicted at
Pensacola after re-work and new paint job and resplendent in
'Chuting Stars' livery. It was after service in Korea that it joined the
US Navy Parachute Team in June 1961. Its new c/n was 43308.
(US Navy)

Chuting Stars

It was 1911 when the US Navy entered aviation. In 1961 to help celebrate the golden anniversary of naval aviation – 'Golden year of the golden wings' the US Navy formed a parachute exhibition team and christened it the 'Chuting Stars'.

The team was composed of volunteer naval parachutists who had been engaged on research and development (R&D) test jumping at the Naval Parachute Facility at El Centro, California.

Leader of the team was Lt jg Mel Greenup from Sonora, California, a veteran smoke jumper from the US Forest Service, with more than 230 jumps to his credit. He was assisted by Chief Warrant Officer Lewis T. Vinson from Canoga Park, California, who was called back to service at his own request to help form the 'Chuting Stars'. CWO Vinson was one of the truly 'greats' in the field of parachuting having made more than 960 jumps.

Three other members had over 300 jumps to their credit, while two more had over 200, one with 165 and one with only 55. When in action performing, the 'Chuting Stars' baled out of their blue and gold Douglas R4D-8 Super DC-3 at 12,500 feet. The team then free fell two miles through space trailing red, white and blue, and blue and gold smoke. During this 60 second plunge, the 'Chuting Stars' attained speeds of two miles a minute, while performing acrobatics, criss-crossing and passing batons in mid-air.

In the two seconds it took the parachute to open, the jumpers slowed their rate of descent from 120 miles an hour, to less than 15 miles an hour. The jumpers then steered their chutes so as to land in a target area in front of the spectators.

Naval Aviation News
1961

Douglas C-47A-80-DL Skytrain 43-15208 c/n 19674 was delivered
on 18 February 1944 serving in Europe with both the US 8th & 9th
Air Forces from 11 April. After World War 2 it went into storage at
Oberpfaff near Munich on 1 January 1948. It was withdrawn for
service during the Berlin Airlift being based at Fassberg as a 'hack'
transport, then home of Douglas C-54 Skymaster squadrons. With its
wartime unit markings etc removed it was named *Fassberg Flyer* as
seen in this photo. It is seen parked at Fassberg with its crew on the
pierced steel planking. In 1950 this Skytrain was transferred to the
Royal Norwegian Air Force. *(AP Publications)*

Berlin Airlift
21 June 1948 to 23 September 1949

The humanitarian Berlin Airlift began on 21 June 1948. It was initiated to defeat the blockade which had been gradually imposed by the USSR upon the three Western sectors of the city. For political purposes, the Russians had suspended all traffic by road, rail and inland waterway between Berlin and the Western Zone of Germany, which was controlled by France, the United Kingdom and the USA.

First signs that the Western Sector of Berlin might have to rely entirely upon an air freight service for its existence were noticed in the spring of 1948, and it was in April that plans were made for meeting such a contingency

Operation 'Knicker' was put into operation on the morning of 24 June 1948. The six RAF Dakotas plied between Wunstorf in Hanover and RAF Gatow in the British sector of Berlin. They carried between them a daily load of 60 tons of food and other essential supplies, and most people accepted the service as a supplementary one to the normal road, rail and canal supply routes, which would last perhaps a few days – until repairs, which the Russians said they were carrying out to the railway line, were completed.

But hardly had 'Knicker' begun when the situation worsened, and a more elaborate freight service took its place, and four days later 'Knicker' became 'Carter Paterson' and three weeks later 'Plainfare.'

It was 26 June when 32 C-47 Skytrain flights from the USAF air base at Wiesbaden hauled 80 tons of supplies into the huge airfield at Tempelhof in the heart of the city. The United States Air Force (Europe) had less than 100 C-47s based at various places many belonging to the European Air Transport Service (EATS) which flew an airline type logistic service in Europe.

Within three weeks the 60th Troop Carrier Group of the USAF had mustered 105 C-47 transports, but the C-54 Skymaster was available and found more suitable and so bore the brunt of the United States effort in the airlift. By 1 October 1948 the Skytrain was withdrawn, leaving the RAF to operate the Dakota into RAF Gatow and the new airfield in the French zone, Tegel. The US operated their task under Operation 'Vittles.'

In mid September 1948 the RAF Dakota force based at Lubeck was augmented by the arrival of twelve Dakota crews of No.1 (Dominion) Squadron, Royal Australian Air Force. In October ten Dakota crews of No.2 (Dominion) Squadron South African Air Force followed, and finally three Dakota crews from the Royal New Zealand Air Force arrived in November the latter crews attached to their RAAF counterparts. All the Commonwealth crews flew many sorties in RAF Dakotas and operated continuously until the end of the airlift as part of the Dakota force, making an extremely valuable contribution to the success of Operation 'Plainfare.'

As the daily airlift tonnage requirement grew, it was soon realized that sufficient military aircraft could not be spared to provide the necessary lifting capacity. For this reason, civilian aircraft were chartered to bridge the gap. Owing to the number of separate companies now involved, it was decided that British European Airways (BEA) should provide liaison officers in Germany through whom the RAF could channel instructions to the operating companies, to deal with both administrative problems and keep records on which payments to the companies could be based. Nearly 20 civil Dakotas from six charter companies plus BOAC were utilised. Payloads of individual Dakotas varied, the problem being solved by 16 August 1948 when all civilian Dakotas began operating with a 7,480 lb payload.

Six RAF Dakotas commenced the airlift on 24 June, 1948 followed two days later by 32 flights by C-47 Skytrains from Wiesbaden flying into Tempelhof with 80 tons of supplies. Within weeks the Allies created a bridge across the sky that won the battle for the hearts – and bellies – of 2.5 million Berliners.

CIVIL DAKOTA STATISTICS FOR THE BERLIN AIRLIFT

Contractor	Reg.	Sorties	Flying Time	Period	Remarks
Air Contractors	C-AIWC	172	466.44	4 Aug 48 – 10 Nov 48	G-AGWS. Flew on D-Day as C-47-DL 41-38749 29th TCSq, 313 TCGrp Folkingham, Lincs.
	G-AIWD	53	154.35		
	G-AIWE	161	445.30		
Air Transport Charter	G-AJVZ	205	562.10	4 Aug 48 – 10 Nov 48	G-AJAY. As KG616 towed gliders on D-Day. 512 Squadron
British Nederland Air Services	G-AJZX	76	230.03	21 Sep 48 – 14 Nov 48	
B.O.A.C.	G-AGIZ	21	58.11	21 Oct 48 – 25 Nov 48	
	G-AGNG	33	89.38		
	G-AGNK	27	76.21		
Ciros Aviation	G-AIJD	91	268.48	6 Aug 48 – 10 Nov 48	
	G-AKJN	237	661.39		
Hornton Airways	G-AKLL	108	301.25	24 Sep 48 – 18 Nov 48	
Kearsley Airways	G-AKAR	84	234.35	4 Aug 48 – 20 Nov 48	
	G-AKDT	162	445.22		
Scottish Airlines	G-AGWS	51	126.29	4 Aug 48 – 27 Aug 48	
	G-AGZF	50	127.45		
Sivewright Airways	G-AKAY	32	87.06	19 Oct 48 – 15 Nov 48	
Trent Valley Av.	G-AJPF	186	504.25	4 Aug 48 – 10 Nov 48	
Westminster Airways	G-AJAY	44	127.10	4 Aug 48 – 23 Nov 48	
	G-AJAZ	184	527.55		

As 41-38749 D-Day with 29th TCSq, 313 TCGrp, Folkingham, Lincs.

As KG616 towed gliders on D-Day with 512 Squadron.

LEFT:
FL597 with 511 Squadron.

BELOW:
KG773 with 525 Squadron.

RIGHT:

As a fitting tribute to the aircraft and personnel who contributed to the Berlin Airlift, two of the Douglas workhorse transports are today permanently on display at Tempelhof, Berlin. The C-54 Skymaster is 45-557 c/n 36010 and the C-47 Skytrain is 45-951 c/n 34214 in European Air Transport Service (EATS) livery. It has had a chequered career being based in Jamaica as a WC-47 with MATS All-Weather Service. After a period in storage at Davis-Monthan, Arizona it was sold as N73856 to Aero American Corp. On 23 April 1962 it went to the Spanish Air Force, being surplus to requirements in 1977. On 14 March 1984 it was registered G-BLFL to Aces High at Duxford going to the USAF on 28 October 1986. *(USAF)*

BELOW:

Using an Aldis signal lamp, an RAF signaller from Air Traffic Control guides a RAF Dakota as it taxis from its dispersal to the duty runway for take-off from an RAF base in Germany which supported the Berlin Airlift. In the background a fleet of RAF Dakotas await their cargo load to be flown into RAF Gatow in the British Zone of Berlin. *(Air Ministry)*

On 21 June 1948 with the blockade of Berlin by the USSR a massive airlift was commenced by the USAF (Europe) and the RAF to keep the beleagured city supplied with necessities including food and coal. By 26 June thirty-two C-47 flights from Wiesbaden had carried eighty tons of supplies into Tempelhof. Within three weeks the USAF had mustered no less than 105 C-47 transports many from the European Air Transport Service (EATS) others from the 60th Troop Carrier Group. Photo shows a daily scene at Tempelhof with USAF C-47s being unloaded. *(Douglas)*

OVERLEAF:
The Commonwealth Air Forces became involved in the Berlin Airlift with the RAAF sending 12 Dakota crews to Lubeck on 15 September 1948 followed by similar contingents from New Zealand and South Africa a month later. The South African party consisted of ten crews comprising 21 officers and 10 NCOs under the command of Major D.M. van der Kaay. Depicted is a SAAF crew – Lt Jack Hosking, Lt Peter Norman-Smith and Lt Attie Basie who flew a total of 140 sorties to Gatow, Berlin between them. The Dakota is 'NU-P' from 240 OCU based at RAF Dishforth, Yorks. The number '83' on the fin is the airlift ident for loading purposes. *(AP Publications)*

Korea

25 June 1950 to 27 July 1953

As the Sunday which was 25 June 1950 dawned there was little to mark it different from any other first day of the week. Over most of Japan the weather was fine, except that it was hot and there was scattered showers and indications that the summer monsoon season was beginning. Over across the Sea of Japan on the peninsular of Korea the Communist North Korean People's Army were watching the weather. Taking advantage of the cover of bad weather, the Red Koreans had drawn up their army along the 38th parallel, and at 0400 hrs on 25 June 1950 they launched a sudden and all-out attack against the Republic of Korea. When the North Koreans struck, said General MacArthur, they 'struck like a cobra'.

On the following day President Truman ordered the US Air Force to the assistance of South Korea. The immediate responsibility of the US Far East Command based in Japan was to provide for the safety of US nationals in Korea. For the air-evacuation mission General MacArthur had charged FEAF to furnish such air-transport aircraft as might be required. The US 5th Air Force under General Partridge ordered all his wing commanders to prepare all available aircraft. Colonel John M. Price, commander of the 8th Wing marshalled his own fleet of aircraft which included three C-47 Skytrains. By 27 June, having received the evacuation order, a further eleven C-47s came from the FEAF base flights and from the Far East Air Materiel Command. A message on 30 June requested more aircraft and personnel, including 15 C-47s needed to haul cargo into smaller Korean airfields. By 7 July a decision was made for the FEAF to reform the 374th Troop Carrier Group to include one squadron of C-47s, this being the 21st Troop Carrier Squadron.

General Bill Tunner, a veteran of the Hump route into China during World War 2 and also organiser of the flights into Berlin during the humanitarian airlift, organised the FEAF Combat Cargo Command which on 20 October 1950 launched the 187th Airborne Regiment Combat Team using 87 C-119s and 40 C-47s dropping 2,860 paratroops and 300 tons of supplies north of Pyongyang. By December the transport C-47s were involved in battle operating with the 1st Marine Air Wing, whilst sorties by the 21st Troop Carrier Squadron were mounting assisted by C-47 Dakotas from the Royal Hellenic Air Force detachment who were new to the theatre. Airdrops of supplies were successful and during December 313 C-119s and 37 C-47s had dropped over 1,580 tons of supplies and equipment.

Early in December 1950 'Kyusha Gypsy' C-47s shuttled some 4,689 wounded or frost-bitten UN soldiers and US Marines from the Communist besieged airstrips at Hagaru-ri and Koto-ri. The 1st US Marine Division had been trapped in the Chosin Reservoir area and were flown out from the Hagaru airstrip. The C-47s could handle 26 patients. At Pupyong-ni C-47s picked up wounded US Marines and flew them over some of Korea's highest mountains to a seaside airstrip at Sokcho-ri. From this strip Rescue helicopters shuttled the casualties to the hospital ship *Consolation* anchored two miles off shore. This exercise of using a hospital ship was terminated on 24 January 1952 as it was felt the wounded were being moved too many times.

Air evacuation proved safe. Only six patients were lost in a single fatal accident on 22 December 1952 when the pilot of a Royal Hellenic Air Force Dakota evidently mistook instructions and collided with a jet fighter-bomber at Suwon air base.

The long Korean conflict eventually reached a stalemate in May 1953 and on 27 June an armistice was agreed. Korea was one of the most controversial of wars. From its growth and experience during the Korean hostilities the fledgling United States Air Force emerged as a power better able to maintain peace through preparedness.

During 1954/55 the Republic of Korea Air Force was supplied with a small number of C-47 Skytrains from USAF stocks. This VC-47D-1-DK 43-48301 c/n 25562 was on loan to Korea from the US 5th Air Force and is seen parked at Sachon air base (K-4) during 1951. It is named *Formosa* and was handed over on 7 January 1951. It was returned to the USAF in September 1954 until 1965 when it was modified to AC-47 gunship configuration and between December 1977 and November 1980 served with the Philippine Air Force and named *Apache Brave*. (Boardman C. Reed)

BELOW:
Post World War 2 one of the many C-47 Skytrain variants was the RC-47 fitted with cameras for aerial reconnaissance. The variant was also used in Korea for flare dropping. Depicted is RC-47D-DK 42-92073 c/n 11833 heavily modified with camera ports in the nose, tail and side fuselage sections and fitted with a dustbin type radar scanner in the forward fuselage. The transport is heavily camouflaged and photo was taken on 22 November 1948. The transport was delivered in June 1943. After USAF service it was placed in storage at the huge Davis-Monthan AFB storage depot in Arizona where it was broken up in June 1967 and the fuselage was put up for sale on 12 September 1967. (Robert F. Dorr)

ABOVE:
On 26 November 1950 a number of C-47 Dakota transports from Flight 13 of the Royal Hellenic Air Force were seconded to Korea to assist the USAF 21st 'Kyusha Gypsy' Squadron euipped with C-47 Skytrains. Transports from Greece included 92-620' named *Jupiter*: and 92-622 *Neptune*. Depicted parked on pierced steel planking (PSP) is 92-622 coded 'E for Echo' with 'NEPTUNE' on the nose. *(AP Publications)*

LEFT:
US ground troops in Korea affectionately called flare-dropping C-47s 'The Old Lamplighters of the Korean Hills'. The Mk.VIII flares, each of which detonated at 5,500 ft, provided four to five minutes of near-daylight illumination. The 3rd Wing modified six C-47s for flare dropping and later in the conflict 'Firefly' coded C-47s frequently searched out and illuminated targets for Douglas B-26 intruder bombers. Photo depicts C-47 crew members preparing flares for an air drop. *(Boardman C. Reed)*

EC-47N-5-DK 43-48871 c/n 26132/14687 *Tijuana Taxi* 1 Sp Op Sq 14 SOW Pleiku, December 1967.

EC-47N-75-DL 42-100950 c/n 19413 *Miss Audrey* Pleiku, December 1967. S.Viet AF.

RC-47N-30-DK 43-48153 c/n 25414/13969 *The Rogue* Pleiku, December 1967.

C-47B-35-DK 44-77152 c/n 33484/16736 *Gunfighter Airlines* Da Nang, March 1968. Support Transport for 366th TFWg equipped with F-4E. *(Robert Mikesh)*

Vietnam

The US Air Force became involved in French Indo-China as early as January 1953 when the US Military Adviser & Assistance Group (MAAG) sent in a team to help the French maintain their C-47 Skytrains, some of which had been drawn from US military reserve stocks. When France gave independence to Vietnam on 12 February 1955 a small air force was formed in South Vietnam with two C-47 squadrons and MAAG took over the training. Viet Cong activities increased steadily until November 1961 when the USAF supplied further aircraft, including four C-47s in South Vietnamese Air Force markings to carry supplies to remote outposts. By 1963 six C-47s had been supplied and USAF aircrews were assigned to help the Vietnamese. With night activity by the Viet Cong, C-47s were used experimentally to drop flares for target illumination, commencing in February 1962. In that month a USAF SC-47 on a psychological warfare leaflet mission was shot down and this made close air support a necessity.

Armament for the C-47 originated with ten 30 calibre machine-guns in the passenger windows, these being replaced by three General Electric 7.62mm Miniguns, firing a total of 18,000 rounds a minute. These were aimed using lateral sights, as the aircraft circled the target in a 30 degree bank. Flares with an illuminating power of 2 million candlepower were used to light up the targets and the AC-47 gunships then orbited at 3,000 ft sometimes lower at a fixed speed of 125 knots. The remote sights were then used to concentrate fire on selected targets. Two AC-47 transports were modified with conversion kits in Vietnam and flight tested in December 1964. They were assigned to the 1st Air Commando Squadron and became known as 'Dragonships' as they spat fire. The AC-47s also acted as Forward Air Controllers and in addition dropped supplies and leaflets. Further C-47s held in storage at Davis-Monthan AFB in Arizona were modified by Air International, Miami, and the miniguns fitted at Forbes AFB, Kansas. The 4th Air Commando Squadron then flew its 20 FC-47s – as they were initially designated – to Vietnam via Hawaii on 23 November 1965. They remained attached to the US 2nd Air Division until 8 March 1966 when the 14th Air Commando Wing was formed.

On 1 August 1968 the 14th Special Operations Wing was formed, with a wide variety of different Skytrain types which included AC-47, EC-47N, EC-47P, EC-47Q the latter specially fitted with electronic countermeasure (ECM) gear and three Tactical Electronic Warfare units. The AC-47s served with the Special Operations Squadrons (SOS) with up to six gunships based at Da Nang, Pleiku, Bien Hoa, Can Tho and Nha Trang.

As progress was made in the development of USAF gunships the AC-47s were supplemented by Fairchild AC-119s and Lockheed AC-130s and most of the USAF C-47s were either retired from service or passed on to friendly air forces. Most AC-47s went to the South Vietnamese Air Force, but as the country soon fell under Communist domination from the north, many transports were flown out to Thailand, where some remain today, whilst others went to the Philippine Air Force.

Vietnam provided the swan song for the venerable C-47 as far as the US Air Force was concerned, and from then on the type was only operated in very small numbers.

Navy in Vietnam

The DC-3 was no stranger to the airspace over Vietnam. In 1965/66, US Navy Headquarters Support Activity, Saigon, operated four vintage transports, two C-47 Skytrains, a U-16 Albatross and a Beechcraft C-45. They formed a bush airline known as 'Air Cofat'. Cofat was a former French cigarette factory in Saigon that became the headquarters of the activity. Cofat's primary mission was airlift support for the Naval Advisory Group in the US Military Assistance Command. Its secondary mission was airlift support for military advisory and Seabee teams. Advisers working with Republic of Vietnam troops in mountain, jungle and rice-paddy enclaves owed their existence to air support, because the Viet Cong made road transport hazardous.

Air Cofat's planes ranged out to fields in all the battle zones, most of them just dirt strips in the jungle or marshy deltas. One C-47 airlifted two-and-a-half tons of lumber and building materials to one Montagnard tribe that had fought its way out of a Viet Cong encirclement and set up a new village in the central highlands.

Danger was a constant companion. An engine fire nearly forced one of the Skytrains down in the trackless highlands but it limped into the strip at Ban Me Thuot with USAF planes flying cover. While a new engine was being installed, crew members joined Army Special Forces and Montagnard tribesmen in security sweeps around the airstrip.

In 1968, one 16-year-old workhorse, a Skytrain converted in 1952 from a C-47, was the only aircraft assigned to Naval Support Activity, Da Nant. The 18-member team of Navy officers and enlisted men fondly called it *Bouncing Bertha*. It supported Army, Navy and Marine Corps personnel in the field. It carried supplies to Seabee outposts, Vietnamese refugees to secure locations, emergency stocks of blood and medical equipment to outlying aid stations and, often, minesweeping, explosive ordnance and underwater demolition teams on short notice.

Although it did not fly on combat missions, it had more than its share of close calls. It was patched up more than once after being struck by shrapnel and ground fire – and kept on flying. Sister aircraft in similar fashion racked up hundreds of flight hours each month over Vietnam.

Helen Collins
Naval Aviation News

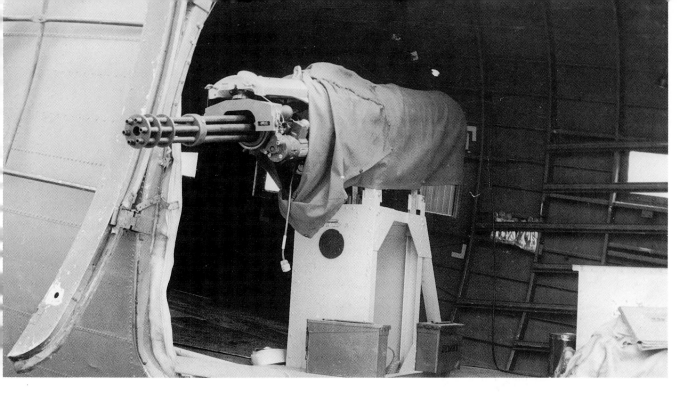

Venerable C-47 Skytrain transports configured as attack aircraft proved highly successful in a new unconventional role in the Vietnam conflict. Equipped with three side-firing General Electric 7.62mm Miniguns (above) each with the capability of firing at a maximum rate of 6,000 rounds per minute. The aging, incongruous warhorse was camouflaged and retained its dignity with the combat designation AC-47, original FC-47, this typifying its attack mission. It was capable of laying down a greater rate of fire-power onto a designated area than any other aircraft, ancient or modern, in the USAF Vietnam inventory. Photo below depicts the miniguns and wire guard fitted to the first FC-47 named *Puff* which was a C-47B-5-DK 43-48579 c/n 25840/14395 sent out to Vietnam with the 1st Air Commando Squadron. The above photo depicts AC-47B-30-DK 44-76722 c/n 33054/16306 gunship based with the 1st Special Operations Squadron, 14th Special Operations Wing. The aircraft was aptly named *Spooky* and carried the unit code 'EN' on the tail. It was seen at Pleiku during December 1967. *(M. Custance)*

As time went by, the AC-47 gunships in Vietnam were supplemented by Fairchild AC-119 and Lockheed AC-130 gunships. Most C-47s in many different configurations were retired from USAF service and passed over to friendly military air arms. Most of the AC-47s went to the Vietnamese Air Force, but as the country fell quickly under Communist domination from the north many transports were flown out to Thailand, others going to the Philippine Air Force. Depicted are C-47 Skytrains of the South Vietnam Air Force – C-47B-20-DK 43-49783 c/n 27044 ex EC-47P of a USAF Tactical Electronic Warfare Squadron and AC-47B-1-DK 43-48491 c/n 25752.

(Norman Taylor)

ABOVE:
A USAF C-47 Skytrain seen flying over a Viet Cong infested area along the Republic of Vietnam coast. The air is filled with psychological warfare leaflets designed to persuade insurgents to turn themselves in. During and after the New Year holiday season in January 1966 more than 1,600 Viet Cong defected, using war leaflets as safe conduct passes. This C-47 operated with the 14th Special Operations Wing in Vietnam. The aircraft went to the Bishop Museum in Honolulu, Hawaii and is 43-49852 c/n 27113. *(USAF)*

LEFT:
During the conflict in Indo-China in the 1950s the French Air Force (Armée de l'Air) operated more than 100 C-47 Dakotas, these equipping Group de Transport 2/15 at Saigon: GT 2/62 'Franche Comte' at Haiphong and Hanoi: GT 1/64 'Bearn' and GT 2/63 'Senegal' at Nhatrang plus GT 1/25 'Tunisie'. All units were equipped with 25 to 30 Douglas transports. Twelve Dakotas remained with Escadrille de Liaisons Aériennes 52 (ELA 52) at Saigon until 1958. Depicted is C-47B-13-DK 43-49049 c/n 26310 coded 'J' from GT 2/63 'Senegal' on an airstrip in Indo-China. It joined the unit in June 1954 using the radio call-sign 'FRANQ'. On 18 March 1967 it went to the Israeli Air Force. *(SIRPA 'AIR')*

ABOVE:
A Cambodian soldier sits on his hammock inside his 'home' which is the tail section of a derelict C-47/DC-3 transport located inside the military compound at Kampong Cham, some 45 miles north-east of Phnom Penh, Cambodia. The origin of the transport is not known. Date of photo is quoted as 10 June 1970. *(Associated Press)*

RIGHT:
An AC-47 Skytrain crew loading Mk.24 flares. On the command of the pilot the loadmaster drops the flares overboard. Each flare had a 24-million candlepower capability. This type of operation was included in the Special Operation Forces in Vietnam. *(USAF)*

British European Airways was officially formed on 1 August 1946 with leased aircraft from BOAC. On 1 February 1947 Railway Air Services with its Dakotas was included, resulting in about 70 Dakotas owned and leased up until May 1963. Depicted at Northolt is G-AMNV c/n 33581 *Sir Eric Geddes* being loaded with cargo. It served BEA between 16 January 1952 to 20 June 1962. Today this DC-3 is a survivor being re-engined with turbo-props at Oshkosh in 1991 and today is registered A2-ADL in Botswana where it operated previously fitted with long nose and tail magnetometers.
(British European Airways)

RIGHT:
A survivor today is this early C-47-DL ex 42-15876 c/n 7393 delivered on 30 July 1942 serving with the North African Wing of Air Transport Command a year later. It returned to the USA on 23 December 1944, being re-assigned to the Caribbean Wing of ATC. It was initially leased then bought by Hawaiian Airlines as N15576 in 1949 and with all but a few of the windows deleted used as a Cargoliner. In 1956 it was sold and became N124E with Libbey Owens Ford Glass Co., Toledo, Ohio. After three owners in Texas it was registered to its current owner M. Ohlinger of McAllen, Texas on 23 June 1978. *(Peter M. Bowers)*

Air Cargo

'**D**uring the middle years of air cargo development – the Thirties and the Forties – there were four major landmarks: Lindbergh's New York to Paris flight; the production of the DC-3; the incredible impact of World War II on aviation development; and finally, the crowning air cargo achievement, the Berlin Airlift. There were numerous other outstanding accomplishments during the period, but these four were elemental to the development of air transport.

The incomparable DC-3. All the words available in many languages have been used to exhaustion for forty years to describe this unique airplane. Perhaps no greater tribute can now be offered than to note than the old 'Gooney Bird' has survived even that supreme trial and still motors monotonously along, performing its manifold duties throughout the world, as reliably and economically as it always has. The Old Lady started life with her nose in the air and all those plaudits haven't changed her attitude a bit.

But the DC-3s are dying one by one – through neglect, replacement, loss of documentation, legal tangles – and when the props stop turning on the last of the working DC-3s, sometime in 1997, the gap they leave behind will be unbridgeable.

The DC-3, in its cargo configuration, was the first airplane to provide the flexible utility, the practicality, the reliability and economy of operation that are necessary to make the transportation of cargo a major and profitable aviation function. Within the considerable range of its capabilities, the DC-3 is yet to be bettered. But the DC-3 began life as a passenger airliner and its usefulness as a cargo carrier remained to be established and proved by the furies of the Second World War.

By the end of the Thirties, two of the three key elements necessary to the full maturation of the air cargo industry were at hand: practical, long-range, payload-carrying aircraft, and basic world-wide navigation and communications systems. The third elements – shippers who could afford to pay for the service – were the governments at war. For the next six years, their demand for air transport was insatiable. Whole fleets of air transports rolled out of the warring nations' assembly plants. The DC-3, fitted with a cargo door and reinforced cargo floor and re-dubbed the C-47 or Dakota, was produced in numbers exceeding 10,000.

The DC-3's big brother, the DC-4 with four engines and four times the DC-3's capacity, followed over distances unprecedented. The Curtiss-Wright C-46 Commando, a fat twin-engined tail-dragger that dwarfed the DC-3, spanned the middle distances. Each of the nations at war produced transport aircraft, but in lesser quantities and most of them are now long forgotten.

The World's training schools taught thousands of young pilots to fly and then dispatched them, with a few hundred hours of experience, in over-loaded aircraft on missions that would test the skill and will of older pilots even today: over the Himalayan "Hump" from India to China; across all the seven seas; into the dismal Arctic. When the war ended, no part of the planet remained unpenetrated by the distant sound of aircraft engines.

By the end of 1945, the world's vast fleets of transport aircraft – far beyond the shrunken transportation needs of a world at peace – were being scrapped or parked in endless ranks under cloudless desert skies. Their young pilots returned to civilian tasks, and unknowingly awaited the culminating test of their war-time lessons – the Berlin Airlift.'

Jim Zeigler
Asia-Plane (Sept 1977)
(Second part of the history of
moving goods by air).

McNeely Air Cargo

'Some dolphins need a ride from Gulfport to an aquarium in Toronto'

'Forty thousand Arkansas chickens have to get to California by sunrise, and an auto plant in Michigan is running out of windshields'

'If Federal Express can't handle it, then McNeely Air Cargo probably can'

'OK, OK. McNeely, based in Earle, Arkansas, doesn't have a high-tech hub, a fleet of jets or a flashy logo. But its pair of creaky, oil-dripping DC-3s will fly almost anything, anywhere, anytime in any weather.'

'One of the rumbling twin-engined planes (N59316 c/n 18986 C-47A-65-DL 42-100523) carried Allied paratroopers on D-Day in 1944. Another (N24320 c/n 20197) ditched into the Mononghela River, Pennsylvania on 22 December 1954 was fished out and rebuilt. Both are more than three decades older than the company's youngest pilot.'

'Company owner Gene McNeely and his other pilots simply cinch their seatbelts tight, put away the coffee mugs and hang on. If an engine fails on take-off, they say they can still climb, and if one stops during a long flight, it only delays their arrival.'

'McNeely says engines on his DC-3s have stopped "five or six times" during the past six years – but no two have ever stopped simultaneously.'

'Maybe that's why he's still here.'

"When an engine goes out, it gives your legs a workout because you have to use the rudder pedals to keep the plane flying straight," he says, "Even under normal conditions you've got to wrestle with the controls to get the plane to do anything."

"Flying a DC-3 is like flying in slow motion. You've got to plan ahead because everything happens real slow."

'Current DC-3 pilots find comfort in their rugged reputation. On a flight to Puerto Rico, a McNeely crew guided its DC-3 through the Bermuda Triangle on Friday the 13th at night. "These planes don't believe in ghosts and neither do we," McNeely scoffs.'

'Another crew took a DC-3 and an extra engine to Alaska for the summer. The plane was used to haul fish to canneries from remote camps.'

"We would land on the beach, fill it up with a load of salmon and take off again," he said.

'We brought the extra engine so that we wouldn't be grounded if one broke down."

'McNeely employs 10 pilots, three mechanics and three clerks. In addition to the DC-3s, McNeely's 8-year-old company owns two more modern twin-engined planes. But his pilots prefer the Gooneybirds.'

'But McNeely said he has no plans to upgrade the engines in his DC-3s anytime soon.'

"These things are too new for new engines. This baby's only got 20,000 hours on it."

'That's not even close to a record. A Boston commuter airline recently retired a DC-3 (N136PB c/n 1997) that had logged 95,000 hours – or almost 11 years in the air.'

"The DC-3 has earned a place in history, and it still has a niche today," McNeely says proudly.

"My planes can get to Seattle in 12 hours and Miami in six. They're reliable, they are sturdy, and, in their own way, they're kind of pretty. I have no doubt they'll outlive you and me both."

Dave Hirschman
Scripps Howard News Service
Arkansas Democrat
Sunday, 29 April 1990.

ABOVE:
General Air Cargo, later General Airways, commenced passenger and freight charters in 1947. Depicted is DC-3 N4112 c/n 26216 which went to General in 1952 and seen parked at Oakland in California during September 1952. The small fleet of DC-3s were named 'Roseliner'. This DC-3 served in Europe with the US 9th Air Force during World War 2 and was finally withdrawn from use at Cuatro Vientos registered EC-ANV in September 1976. *(William T. Larkins)*

LEFT:
The registration of many DC-3s in the USA often changes with each owner, others are the original allocation, as c/n 4715 N86553 depicted. It was built as an early C-47-DL 41-185-0 serving with the US 5th Air Force in Australia and the 13th Air Force in the Pacific. Its first owner after its return to the USA was Delta as N86553 in 1946 with whom it served until 31 March 1963, being used as an air freighter in the latter days. Today still registered N86553 it is with Boringuen Air, San Juan, Puerto Rico. *(AP Publications)*

This immaculate US Army C-47E 45-0972 c/n 34236 served with the US Army Missile Command between April 1972 and May 1976 and was one of three Skytrains based at Redstone Arsenal, Alabama as part of the huge US Army Materiel Command with HQ at Gravelly Point, Washington DC. The transport survives today, being registered N8040L to the New England Escadrille at Cambridge, Massachusetts. It is an ex US Air Force C-47B-45-DK delivered on 25 July 1945.
(AP Publications)

US Army

The creation of the US Air Force on 18 September 1947 left the US Army without a single aircraft capable of carrying a significant outsize cargo load or carrying more than twelve passengers. In the years immediately following 1947 the US Air Force was often unable or reluctant to provide a large aircraft on request from the US Army. The obvious solution to this problem was for the US Army to operate its own medium transport aircraft, but again the USAF was extremely reluctant to sanction the required exception to the 5,000 lb gross weight limitation when the US Army proposed its plan.

However, the US Air Force's inability to consistently provide required on-call transport aircraft support ultimately forced it to agree to the US Army's proposal. The C-47 Skytrain was chosen for US Army use for several reasons: there were plenty of C-47 transports available: the type was robust and well-suited to the sort of rough field conditions often encountered by US Army aircraft: and, almost certainly, because senior US Air Force leaders felt that the US Army's operation of an elderly and – apparently – obsolescent type would not seriously detract from the US Air Force's image.

The first C-47 Skytrain aircraft were transferred from the USAF to the US Army in the early 1950s, and during the following two decades the latter service operated nearly 40 Skytrain transports. The majority were ex US Navy R4D- variants, while the remainder were former USAF examples.

The C-47 Skytrain served the post-war US Army long and well in a wide variety of roles. Indeed the US Army can claim to be the last of the US armed services to operate the venerable Gooney Bird with the last US Army Skytrain ex US Navy C-47H BuNo.12436 c/n 9619 being retired to the US Army Aviation Museum at Fort Rucker, Alabama in 1982.

Majority of the transports were used for general support duties but some operated fitted with sophisticated electronic equipment. They were based at Kwajalein test site in the Pacific with the Army's Missile Command, whilst at least two were used by the 'Golden Knights' Army parachute demonstration team. Several were the higher powered C-47E which had R-20000 engines fitted. Others were fitted with wing racks for carrying test equipment such as flares etc. One had external wing tanks and another was fitted with radar including Sideways-Looking Airborne Radar (SLAR). The designation NC-47B was applied to these unique Skytrain transports fitted with electronics etc.

One of the first C-47s to join the US Army was US Navy R4D-7 BuNo.99848 c/n 33299 during August 1956. Six other US Navy R4D transports were removed from storage at Litchfield Park in Arizona. They were made serviceable and flown to the old Mirana AFB just north of Tucson and after a short inspection for acceptance were flown to Dallas, Texas. Here Executive Aircraft Service stripped down each aircraft to the bare rivets and rebuilt them. They were powered by Pratt & Whitney R-1830-94 engines with the two-stage blower giving high altitude for some of the US Army projects. Airstair doors were installed plus undercarriage doors. Some had a 28-ft SLAR antenna fitted under the fuselage. Three went to Fort Monmouth, New Jersey; these being 39103 c/n 32818, 50761 c/n 26273 and 99831 c/n 33170. Another three were assigned to Fort Huachuca, Arizona – 12444 c/n 9757, 17220 c/n 13318 and 50814 c/n 26718. Remmert-Werner in St. Louis, Missouri were also involved in US Army contracts involving the new C-47 and modifications required. A USAF transport was 43-16277 c/n 20743 an ex Air Rescue transport so fitted with cabin heaters and had a 1,600 gallon fuel capacity. It went to Texas Instruments to have a SLAR antenna fitted.

The unique project was coded 'Operation Shirley'.

TOP LEFT:
Red River Army Depot, Texarkana, Texas.

TOP RIGHT:
JFK Center for Mil Assistance, Fort Bragg, North Carolina.

MIDDLE:
Flight Training Center, Fort Stewart, Georgia.

RIGHT:
Electronics Command, Fort Monmouth, New Jersey.

United Nations

Established as a successor to the League of Nations, the United Nations Charter was signed at San Francisco on 26 June 1945, its main objective being the maintenance of peace and its six principal organs are the General Assembly, Security Council, Secretariat at New York, the International Court at The Hague, Economic & Social Council and Trusteeship Council. Acronyms used by the United Nations on their DC-3/C-47 transports include 'U.N.R.W.A.' United Nations Relief and Works Agency, 'U.N.R.R.A.' United Nations Relief and Rehabilitation Administration, 'U.N.O.' United Nations Organisation, 'U.N.E.S.C.O.' United Nations Educational, Scientific & Cultural Organisation, 'U.N.I.C.E.F.' United Nations International Children's Emergency Fund.

The C-47 Dakota has been a workhorse for the United Nations, and has been in service with UN missions in Indonesia, Greece, Palestine, India, Pakistan, in the Gaza Strip and Sinai Desert and in the Congo, not forgetting the Lebanon. All these missions had at least one aircraft – the Congo mission had no less than ten in service at one time. The aircraft were used on a variety of tasks, mainly carrying passengers and freight plus duties as an ambulance and observation transport. The Royal Canadian Air Force, the US Air Force, Italian Air Force provided military C-47 Dakotas, whilst other countries such as Sweden supplied DC-3s. All aircraft were finished in an overall white finish and allocated a UN number, whilst the crews wore the blue beret and UN badge.

No.115 Air Transport Unit – United Nations – was based at El Arish, Egypt and on 17 June 1958, an RCAF Dakota Mk.IV KN666 in full UN livery was forced by United Arab Republic MiG-15 jets to land at Abu Suer, allegedly for not flying the established air corridor. Other Dakotas used by No.115 ATU were RCAF Mk.IVs 656, 989, 563 and 511. In July 1964, the Dakotas were replaced by Caribou transports at several of the UN missions.

Following the withdrawal from the Congo of Belgian military forces and during the subsequent war in 1963-65 the United Nations leased up to 20 Dakotas for varied operations with the peace-keeping force. Some came from the US Air Force and others from civil operators such as Transair-Sweden. Their subsequent fates after UN service is vague, some being returned to their owners, whilst others such as the US Air Force C-47s being sold locally to operators in Africa or for spares to support Air Congo transports. The UN numbering system was retained in the '200' series with 'UN-201 to UN-220' recorded.

In May 1993 two DC-3s from New Zealand were employed under a United Nations contract to distribute food in Cambodia; these two aircraft being numbered 'UN-280' and 'UN-281' and finished in the standard white overall finish. During 1946/47 four Royal Australian Air Force Dakotas operated in China with UNRRA.

Scene at Boende airstrip in the Congo on 5 April 1962 as local residents watch the activity connected with the arrival of United Nations C-47 '200'. The transport brought stocks of badly needed medicines for use in the area, and was attached to the ONUC air mission, the second, to the Province of Equateur. This aircraft was ex C-47A-35-DL 42-23918 c/n 9780 delivered June 1943 to the USAAF and in 1953 was a EC-47A with the US 10th Air Force. In 1966 after UN use it went to Air Congo as 9Q-CUD crashing on 19 February 1970. *(United Nations)*

ABOVE:
During 1954 when all was unrest in the Middle East, the United Nations force in the troubled area was at full strength operating a wide variety of vehicles, personnel of many nations and aircraft which included the Dakota. Depicted is Dakota '75640' which we cannot identify on one of its three-times-a-week flights to the Gaza Strip in Egypt. This is the only link with the outside world, except for the long desert train ride through the Nile Valley. Most of the Dakotas used during this period were from the Royal Canadian Air Force. *(United Nations)*

LEFT:
The United Nations Emergency Force (UNEF) in the Middle East was based at El Arish, Egypt in the late 1950s with No.115 Air Transport Unit (UN) with aircraft and crews supplied by the Royal Canadian Air Force. On 17 June 1958 a RCAF Dakota Mk.IV KN666 was forced by United Arab Republic MiG-15 jets to land at Abu Suer allegedly for not flying the established air corridor. Seen parked at El Arish in May 1959 is a RCAF de Havilland Otter '3745' and RCAF Dakota 656 ex C-47A-40-DL 42-23970 c/n 9832 delivered to RCAF 14 July 1943 and serving with the United Nations both in the Middle East and the Congo between 1958 and July 1964. *(United Nations)*

The acronym U.N.R.W.A. on this all-white United Nations DC-3 stands for "United Nations Relief & Works Agency" employed on Palestine refugee relief work in the Near East. In 1949 a UN body was established by the UN General Assembly to assist some 750,000 refugees from the former British Mandate Territory of Palestine who lost their homes and livelihoods as a result of the disturbances during and after the creation of the State of Israel. Many nations supplied troops for UN task forces in troubled areas in the Middle East and the Congo, whilst DC-3/C-47 transports came from Canada, Sweden, Italy and the USA. *(AP Publications)*

BELOW:

By August 1960 some 11,500 troops from no less than nine countries were on duty with the United Nation forces in the troubled Republic of the Congo, helping to restore law and order and calm in the country. Assistance from the UN included technical and medical personnel, air transport, food, heavy materials and various supplies. After an inter-tribal fight between the Luluas and Balubas in Kasai province, food was sent by UN Dakota '206' from Leopoldville to Luluabourg the capital of Kasai. The urgently required food supply is seen after being unloaded from the UN Dakota on 10 August 1960. *(United Nations)*

In May 1993 two 50-year-old DC-3s ZK-BBJ c/n 34222 (UN 280) and ZK-AMR c/n 9286 (UN 281) left Ardmore, New Zealand for work with the United Nations in Cambodia. Based at Phnom Penh they were purchased by an Auckland catering company on a contract to supply and deliver food to UN peacekeepers stationed throughout Cambodia. Both DC-3s were painted in the white livery synonymous with United Nations aircraft and vehicles. *(D.A. Noble)*

ABOVE:
The Cairns Airport Authority at Cairns, Queensland, Australia, own this DC-3 which is on display as 'VH-BPA' c/n 12187, it being in Bush Pilots Airways (BPA) livery. It was photographed on 22 September 1993. The aircraft was built in December 1943 going to the RAF as FZ631 on 9 January 1944 and after being ferried to the UK was fitted out as a VIP aircraft for use by Gen. Maitland Wilson and named *Freedom*. After service in Air Command South-East Asia (ACSEA) it went to QANTAS as VH-EAN and after many owners it went to Bush Pilots Airways on 28 October 1981 being put on display in December 1987 with fictitious registration 'VH-BPA.'
(Peter R. Arnold)

RIGHT:
The DC-3/C-47 Skytrain is no stranger to the remote Alaskan air space, for in addition to World War 2 the versatile transport operated in the post-war years, and was resident with the Air National Guard. Today the type is still active as a workhorse. Two Skytrains are preserved in the state, 42-100857 c/n 19320 in the Alaska ANG Museum at Kulis air base at Anchorage, whilst 43-15200 c/n 19666, depicted, is on display at Wasila and belongs to the Alaska Historical & Transportation Museum. Between May 1967 and May 1974 0-315200 served with the 144th Air Transport Squadron, Alaska Air National Guard. *(Michael Prophet)*

126

Museums

The world's aviation museum scene is expanding throughout the world and the acquisition of a suitable DC-3/C-47 remains quite high on the list for inclusion. Some transports are restored and remain static, whilst others are carefully preserved in flying condition and often appear on the air show scene. Others are still involved in a very long term, but methodical, restoration programme by DC-3 enthusiasts and organisations. Over the past two decades many of the major airlines have at long last recognised how the faithful DC-3 served them in their pioneer days, and are searching the backwoods for one of their originals, and when found, restoring it to flying condition often with the help of veteran retirees, the finished product appearing in the livery of the day when it flew the airways in the 1930s.

In the USA alone there are over 70 aircraft museums in 30 states all having at least one DC-3 on its inventory. The number is increasing every year. Private museums are being established in odd corners of North America which includes Canada.

One of the special programmes which increased greatly the number of military C-47 Skytrains on show in the USA was the huge generous USAF Museum Program. For a number of years military air bases had acquired retired military aircraft, including the C-47 to serve as gate-guards, inclusion in the base museum, use as a training aid, memorials etc., but unfortunately there was no central co-ordination. Under US Air Force regulation AFR-2104 all air bases were expected to initiate plans for a base historical museum, all exhibits coming under the jurisdiction of the USAF Museum located at Wright-Patterson AFB., Dayton, Ohio. This official directive has resulted in many new USAF base museums being set up with excellent standards of maintenance being applied to the many C-47 Skytrains administered from the USAF museum at Dayton. Similarly the US Marine Corps and the US Navy have excellent aviation museums which includes well preserved examples of the R4D- Skytrain and Super DC-3.

The situation over the border in Canada is similar in many aspects and the National Aviation Museum was consolidated in 1964 by amalgamating several collections which were moved into new buildings in Rockcliffe, Ontario. The Canadian Warplane Heritage has now become established as one of the major collections, including airworthy warbirds, in North America and has several notable restorations to its credit. The venerable DC-3/Dakota has not been forgotten.

Museums which were launched in the 1960s by volunteer groups are now becoming well established in permanent facilities with a wide and varied selection of aircraft on show. The Canadian Armed Forces are no exception to the rule, and several examples of the Dakota are held on display at air bases throughout the continent. Nearly a dozen museums in Canada now boast the DC-3/Dakota in their collection.

American Airlines DC-3

As American Airlines were mainly responsible for the birth of the DC-3 and the first to operate the Douglas Sleeper Transport, it is more than a fitting tribute that the 'C.R. Smith Museum' located in Dallas, Texas, boasts an early example of the airliner which is today on display outside the excellent museum.

On 11 March 1940, Douglas DC-3-227B NC21798 c/n 2202 and named *Flagship Knoxville* and fitted with a right-hand passenger door finished in American Airlines livery was delivered from the busy factory located at Santa Monica, California. After 53 years and several owners during which it had accumulated more than 50,000 flying hours, *Knoxville* finally returned home to Dallas, Texas, to become a new museum piece.

The veteran DC-3 is one of the 82 original Douglas transports purchased by American Airlines before World War 2.

RIGHT:

The centre-piece of a very busy roundabout in Jeddah is this DC-3 c/n 9623 last registered 5B-CBD in Cyprus. During 1975 it was withdrawn from use in Saudi Arabia and subsequently became one of several derelict DC-3s at the old airport at Jeddah. It being in the most complete condition it was selected and restored by apprentices from the national carrier Saudia-Saudi Arabian Airlines and was finished to represent the DC-3 type which founded the airline in 1945. Despite the engines and nose cone being missing, replacements were skilfully fabricated from wood. *(Barry Dowsett)*

BELOW:

The records indicate that DC-3A OH-VKB c/n 1975 last flew on 27 April 1987 and was then towed from Helsinki airport to the Helsinki Air Museum. It is seen during 1973 fitted with geophysical survey equipment. It is a Fokker-assembled right-hand passenger door DC-3A-214 delivered on 20 August 1937 as SE-BAC *Falken* with Swedish Air Lines. It was purchased by Kar-Air on 12 January 1954 and had the survey equipment fitted in November 1969. *(Paul Zogg)*

It is coincidental that two early DC-3A-197s c/n 1910 and 1911 are today survivors, with one of the USA in flying condition and c/n 1911 in the United Kingdom in the Science Museum collection at Wroughton, Wiltshire. Over the 60 years the DC-3 has always been a show attraction as seen in this photo taken on 31 July 1937 at an air show at Sea Island, Vancouver, Canada depicting DC-3A NC16071 c/n 1911 *Mainliner Los Angeles* being shown to the general public. It was delivered to United on 5 December 1936 serving with the airline until 12 August 1954. It was delivered to Wroughton on 28 November 1978 registered EI-AYO. Hopefully one day it will be restored in United livery as NC16071. *(AP Publications)*

The California 'grizzly bear" emblem has been part of the California ANG insignia since June 1924 when the state gained its first squadron at Santa Monica. Depicted is VC-47A-85-DL 43-15579 c/n 20045 delivered in April 1944, serving with the California ANG from September 1954. Note the lack of US national insignia and it was named *The Grizzly* and by September 1972 it had accumulated 11,614 flying hours. It was acquired by the 144th Air Defense Wing of the Cal ANG in 1968 and was used to transport the then Governor Earl Warren. It ferried VIPs around the state and was used as a flying command post during floods and similar emergencies. By March 1971 it was used briefly by the US Marine Corps and in March 1973 was graciously retired and is preserved at Fresco airport. *(William T. Larkins)*

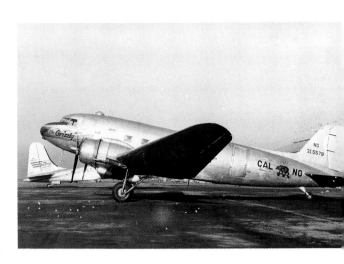

Delivered to Eastern Air Lines as a DC-3-201 NC18124 c/n 2000 on 7 December 1937 the last passenger flight took place on 12 October 1952. The veteran had completed nearly 57,000 hours in the air, equivalent to 6½-years flying nonstop. Captain Eddie Rickenbacker, the President of Eastern presented the transport to the Smithsonian Institute on 1 May 1953. It is depicted being towed up Pennsylvania Avenue at dead of night. On 1 July 1976 it went into the new National Air & Space Museum and resides today alongside such veterans as Lindbergh's *Spirit of St. Louis*. *(AP Publications)*

Survivors

There is no doubt that the DC-3 and its many variants is unique in the number still surviving after six decades. It is very difficult to estimate just how many are serviceable at any one time, and one has to concede to the fact that as each year passes the number is gradually reducing. However here in the Golden Jubilee year it is felt that the figure of 1,000 survivors seems near correct. That includes the 300 plus estimated to be still in use with military air arms all over the world. The workhorse is now getting both difficult, and expensive, to replace. The advent of the turbo-prop version will no doubt help to prolong the life of the Grand 'Ole Lady.

In March 1994 we received an accurate listing from Canada which identified 43 DC-3s still in service and registered. A keen 'reggie spotter' who bravely ventured into South America during October 1994 logged 63 DC-3s. There are currently over 200 registered as flying in the United States. Here in the United Kingdom, Air Atlantique at Coventry operates no less than 11 venerable transports.

The hours flown on DC-3 airframes varies very much, but there is no doubt that shortly the first to attain 100,000 flying hours is forecast. There are several contenders we can identify, all based in North America.

It is fully accepted that the DC-3/C-47 series of transports must be one of the strongest ever designed and built. Time does take its toll and as mentioned earlier each year will see fewer of these venerable classics taking to the air. Parts are becoming difficult to obtain, while inspections and repairs are becoming specialised and costly. The radial engines, be it the Wright Cyclone or the Pratt & Whitney Twin Wasp are being rebuilt over and over again, at a price. Another problem is the availability of 100 octane fuel (AVGAS) which is already non-existent in some parts of the aviation world. There is no lack of volunteers, both male and female, to fly the DC-3 and Air Atlantique has on its books 35 Dakota-rated pilots.

What was a barren hulk yesterday can often be restored to a fully serviceable flying DC-3 today, and with care on rebuild many parts of the aircraft can be given zero time by a qualified inspector, this applying to both airframe and engines. Fortunately most countries have the experience of operating at least one DC-3 or 'Gooney Bird' in one form or another. "Long may she reign."

To the layman there is no external difference between the real civil DC-3, and the military C-47/C-53. The transport depicted carries the original registration NC21729 which identifies it as a DC-3-201B c/n 2141 built for Eastern Air Lines and delivered on 17 June 1939, serving the airline until 12 June 1952 when sold to Purdue Aeronautics. Many owners followed and it was Paul Weske who took its ownership in 1977 gave it its World War 2 Skytrain livery. As 'D8-Z' it represents a transport operated by the 94th Troop Carrier Squadron, 439th Troop Carrier Group, 50th Troop Carrier Wing initially based at Upottery, Devon. Today this original DC-3 is in Canada as C-GDAK with Canucks Unlimited and reputed to have flown well over 80,000 hours. *(Stuart Howe)*

LEFT:
Seen during the 50th Anniversary of D-Day in appropriate livery is F-BLOZ c/n 13142 disguised '115111' coded 'U5-' code letters used by the 81st Squadron, 436th Troop Carrier Group based at Membury, Wiltshire. It is seen at La Ferte Alais, and is apparently airworthy. After a brief return to the USA it returned to France as F-BAXS being leased to Air France and Air Atlas, finally bought by Air France on 27 April 1953. In May 1964 it became F-SEBD later F-BLOZ in 1981. It was originally a C-47A-20-DK 42-93251. *(Peter Berry)*

BELOW:
Expo 86 held in Canada included a DC-3 Airmada held between 5-7 June 1986. Depicted are fifteen of the 24 DC-3s that rallied at Abbotsford Airport, British Columbia, between those dates for the Airmada. They are seen just prior to take-off for the flyby held on 7 June of the 1986 World Exhibition at Vancouver and Vancouver Island. Most of the DC-3s depicted are survivors today for the Diamond Jubilee of a Grand 'Ole Lady, the DC-3. *(Ed Long)*

On 30 April 1994 this South African DC-3 ZS-NJE c/n 9836 ex '6867' of the SAAF arrived in the United Kingdom on completion of a long delivery flight. Finished in World War 2 camouflage it undertook flights in conjunction with the 50th anniversary of D-Day. It is now registered G-BVOL with Airborne Initiative based at Middle Wallop in flying condition. Completed on 8 July 1943 as 42-23974 it went to the RAF under Lend-Lease as FD938 seven days later. It was delivered to the Middle East in August and transferred to 28 Squadron SAAF on 27 August becoming '6867' on 3 October 1945. The interior is today equipped with the original bucket seats etc. *(Frank A. Hudson)*

Depicted in immaculate condition and smart livery is VH-EDC c/n 12874 today a survivor in Bankstown with Southern Pacific who took ownership in February 1993. It was built as a Lend-Lease Dakota A65-45 for the RAAF in April 1944. On 17 November 1949 it was registered VH-JVF with the Dept. of Civil Aviation being re-registered VH-CAR on 14 July 1950. It went to QANTAS on 27 June 1966 who re-registered it VH-EDC. It eventually went to BPA (Papua New Guinea) Pty Ltd. on 8 August 1973. Other owners followed and for a period in 1987 it was in storage at Brisbane. *(AP Publications)*

ABOVE:
Today scenic flights over Sydney are flown from Bankstown, plus tours to the outback, in DC-3 VH-SBL c/n 12056. It is depicted at Bankstown in full 'Dakota National Air' livery on 1 May 1993 with 'Captain Jack Curtis' inscribed under the cockpit. Built as a Lend-Lease Dakota A65-29 for the RAAF it utilised radio call-sign 'VH-CTZ' and in 1946 went to Australian Airlines as VH-TAE. In 1960 it was leased to New Zealand National Airlines, then went to Trans Australia as VH-SBL prior to secondment to New Guinea as P2-SBL and P2-ANR between 1973-76 when it returned as VH-SBL to Australia. In June 1992 it was registered to Peter Starr, Gorsford, New South Wales who is the current owner. *(Peter R. Arnold)*

RIGHT:
Seen shortly after a complete refurbishment OH-LCH is parked at Kruunupyy airport, Finland on 8 August 1984. It is preserved in flying condition by the Finnish Dakota Association (Airveteran Finland) and is an original DC-3A-354 c/n 6346 built for Pan American as NC34953 but impressed into military service at the factory becoming C-53C 43-2003 and delivered on 27 December 1942. It served with the Atlantic and later the European Wing of Air Transport Command in 1943. After storage at Oberpfaff near Munich was sold to Finnair as OH-LCH. A second DC-3 OH-LCD c/n 19309 ex 42-100848 is stored at Helsinki-Vantas airport in poor condition, but could be rebuilt and flown. *(Kari Heikkala)*

LEFT:
Seen parked at Midland, Texas on 7 October 1993 is N227GB c/n 33345 in wartime livery as Skytrain C-47A-80-DL 43-15033 c/n 19499 coded '2L-A' from the 302nd Troop Carrier Squadron 441st Troop Carrier Group based at Merryfield, Somerset on D-Day. The aircraft is actually TC-47B-35-DK 44-77013 which went to the US Navy as a R4D-7 BuNo.99854 which served after World War 2 with CAA/FAA as N32 being bought by the Confederate Air Force on 16 March 1981. Registered on 5 June 1993 to the American Airpower Heritage Flying Museum at Midland. *(Frank A. Hudson)*

BELOW:
The DC-3 was used in New Zealand commencing in the postwar years with New Zealand National Airways Corp, the only company operating scheduled services for any great length of time, or in any numbers. One of the most interesting uses of the DC-3 was its modification as an aerial top-dresser to improve sheep pastures. Another DC-3 was used for the carriage of live deer from hunting areas. Depicted are two DC-3s – ZK-AMR c/n 11970 and ZK-AWP c/n 33135 in Speedlink parcels livery. Both are current and operated in Cambodia with the United Nations. *(Jim Winchester)*

Seen at Tico, Florida on 7 October 1994 is N3239T c/n 19054 immaculate in World War 2 livery representing C-47A-65-DL 42-100591 U5- *Tico Belle* from the 81st Troop Carrier Squadron 436 Troop Carrier Group based at Membury, Wiltshire on D-Day 6 June 1944. Owned by Valiant Air Command since October 1982, the DC-3 normally flies as K-684 in full Danish Air Force livery. After USAAF service in Europe, including storage at Oberpfaff near Munich, it went to the Royal Norwegian Air Force in May 1950 and to the Royal Danish Air Force in 1956. *(Frank A. Hudson)*

This C-47B-15-DK despite showing the serial 43-15174 c/n 19640 an ex 9th Troop Carrier Command Skytrain salvaged on 26 April 1945, is 43-49507 c/n 26768/15323 and today is preserved at the USAF Museum, Wright-Patterson AFB, Dayton, Ohio. It is unique in being the last one of many in USAF service being delivered to the museum on 30 June 1975 from the 834th Tactical Composite Wing based at Hurlburt Field near Eglin, Florida. It had accumulated 20,821 hours and the pilot, Major John Elkin USAF flew his 10,000 hours in this Skytrain. On 19 June 1987 the C-47 was painted as depicted representing 'M2-O-Orange' a C-47A-80-DL from the 88th Troop Carrier Squadron, 438th Troop Carrier Group, 53rd Troop Carrier Wing, initially based at RAF Greenham Common, Berkshire. Photo was taken on 23 June 1987. *(Hugh V. Morgan)*

Classic Air of Zurich-Kloten, Switzerland, has operated DC-3s HB-ISB c/n 4667 and HB-ISC c/n 9995 on pleasure flights since 1986. It was during the 50th anniversary of the DC-3 on 17 December 1985 that the company announced its intention to commence operations with a DC-3. The DC-3 N88YA was purchased by Air Atlantique for spares, but after a period in storage it was rebuilt becoming HB-ISC and registered to Classic Air on 22 September 1986. *(Classic Air)*

LEFT:
A joint venture with the US air charter company Viking Express Inc. is Vintage Airways of Orlanda which consists of two restored DC-3s N12RB c/n 20401 *Amelia* and N22RB c/n 4926 *Eve* which began operating sight-seeing flights from Orlando to Key West in December 1992. The venture is part of Richard Branson's Virgin Group and it is estimated that each DC-3, after extensive renovations, cost $350,000. DC-3 N12RB is an ex Skytrain 43-15935 delivered 29 May 1944 having many owners within the USA, while N22RB is an ex C-53 Skytrooper 42-6474 delivered on 30 April 1942 and again having many previous owners in the USA. Rumour has it that Richard Branson intends to purchase more DC-3s and begin a service to Cuba and Miami, and eventually to bring Vintage Airways to Europe.

(Frank A. Hudson)

This DC-3 F-GEOM c/n 9798 is used for cargo hauling by Stellair. It was destined to be based in the UK with Classic Airways, one of three DC-3s, and registered G-OFON but the proposed operations ceased in the Spring of 1993 due to financial difficulties. Built as a C-47A-30-DL 42-23926 delivered on 1 July 1943 it served in North Africa and in Europe with the US 8th & 9th Air Forces. It served in Czechoslovakia and in France with the Aeronvale being retired in 1983. *(AP Publications)*

With the port wheel about to complete its cycle, Dakota ZA947 c/n 10200 is depicted in the circuit pattern at RAE Bedford on 17 October 1990. It is finished in the raspberry ripple markings adopted for most aircraft operated by units of the Royal Aircraft Establishment. It was originally '661' with the RCAF and as 'KG661' based at RAE West Freugh for many years on trial work. By November 1987 it had flown 12,637 hours and was with the Transport Flight at RAE Farnborough. In April 1993 it was assigned to the Battle of Britain Memorial Flight at RAE Coningsby, Lincolnshire and is today camouflaged and in 271 Squadron marks as 'YS-DM' KG374 as flown by the late David Lord VC. *(RAE Bedford)*

Old and new decades apart at Long Beach with the factory new first MD-11 airliner parked with a 1939 vintage DC-3-313 still with its original right-hand door fitted. It is used today for flying skydivers and is registered N26MA c/n 2169 and operated by the Perris Valley Para Center in California. It was built as NC21781 for Penn Central Airlines and delivered from the Santa Monica factory on 29 November 1939. The DC-3 is today a favourite carriage for skydiving enthusiasts with as many as 40 plus accommodated in the bare fuselage. *(Douglas)*

This transport joined l'Escadrille 56S of the French Aéronvale at Nimes Garon on 6 February 1964 retaining US Navy BuNo.17223 c/n 13321. Used as a navigation trainer and as late as 1982 the unit operated a fleet of 20 C-47 transports. The Dakota was surplus to requirements in 1982 and sold to Basler Flight Services in the USA who ferried it to Oshkosh as N96BF on 30 September 1985 with 10,548 hours on the airframe. Converted to Turbo-67 standard in August 1989 and due to be delivered to Air Colombia, but was retained by Basler as a demonstration aircraft, being demonstrated at the Farnborough Air Show in 1992 and also demonstrated at Air Atlantique at Coventry. *(AP Publications)*

Foreign Air Arms

Over the years the venerable DC-3/C-47 has been involved in political, military, economic and social issues around the globe. It has survived the many differences of race, language, culture and standards of living. International relations, military technology and defence hardware is rarely encountered by the average citizen, but it both defends and threatens him and so cannot be ignored. It is revealed that between 1962 and 1967 world expenditure on arms and associated military services increased 50 per cent. More money was being spent on military hardware than at any time except during World War 2.

Latin America has produced guerrilla movements, born in the 1960s, in Guatamala, Venezuela, Colombia, Peru, Argentina, Brazil and Bolivia, all of which have met with varying degrees of failure. To help the Latin American armies counter the guerrilla threat the United States has supplied aid and training including a quantity of Douglas C-47 transports, some being turbo-prop transports including a number of gunships. These were supplied under the US Department of Defense code name "Operation Peace Turbo" under a 39-page contract with the USAF and Basler Turbo Conversions of Oshkosh, Wisconsin. Initially this was for two AC-47 gunship conversions for El Salvador.

However not all the aid offered was accepted. Military coups in 1968 and Bolivia in 1969, produced a new kind of military dictatorship that proved to be hostile to certain entrenched economic interests in the United States. Today the drug war is still prevalent in many areas of Latin America, often involving the ubiquitous DC-3.

It was World War 2 that introduced the DC-3/C-47 into battle, although both DC-2 and DC-3 transports were earlier involved in the Spanish Civil War and in Finland against the Russians, proving that air transport power had become almost synonymous with military strength. After World War 2 with the recurrent international tensions – the Berlin Airlift being a very good example – plus minor conflicts of the troubled post-war years, resulted not only in the continued growth in importance of military aviation, but also extended the life of any 'sell by date' if there ever was one, of the C-47.

From Angola to Zimbabwe, the Douglas military transport has served faithfully, involving nearly 100 countries and military air arms, and today still serves in 35 of these involving nearly 300 transports. Turkey and South Africa appear to operate the largest fleets with a proportion of the latter being converted to turboprop standard using the high technology gained on the type over 50 years. In fact No.44 Squadron SAAF celebrated its proud history of half a century operating the Dakota from 12 March 1944 to 12 March 1994, and still proudly operates the Grand 'Ole Lady today living up to its motto "Prosumus" which translated means "We are useful."

RIGHT:
Douglas Super DC-3 N31310 c/n 43395 from the Naval Arctic Research Laboratory (NARL) based at Point Barrow in Alaska seen parked in August 1976 at Gambel, an Eskimo settlement on St. Lawrence Island in the Bering Strait between Alaska and the USSR. Established in 1947 the NARL operated the earlier R4D- Skytrain prior to the Super DC-3. *(AP Publications)*

BELOW:
Zimbabwe, the former colony of S. Rhodesia, was re-named on 18 April 1980. The transport element of the armed forces included Dakotas with No.3 Squadron based at Old Sarum the main air base. The first Dakota was supplied to the SRAF in 1947 by the South African Air Force. During 1954/5 a number of ex RAF Dakotas, overhauled by Scottish Aviation, were supplied and more followed in 1964 from South Africa. Today ten are on the inventory but for sale. Depicted is '7310' c/n 42978 ex 3D-ABI built as a post-war DC-3D for Swissair as HB-IRC delivered 15 April 1946 going to the SRAF on 13 May 1977. *(AP Publications)*

The Royal Hellenic Air Force – Elliniki Acropoia – has operated a large fleet of C-47 Dakotas since 1947 of which only a handful remain today. They saw action, firstly in the civil war during 1947 and later with the United Nations in Korea during 1950. Bomb racks were fitted during the civil war, and attacks made on communist-held buildings in Athens and elsewhere. The USA supplied a batch of 30 overhauled C-47s 92612–92641 in 1949 and after Greece joined NATO in 1952 others were supplied. A number of early Greek Dakotas were ex RAF, these retaining their serials after transfer. Depicted is 92626 now retired. *(AP Publications)*

Probably the world's largest operator of the Dakota is the South African Air Force who are today still using approximately 40 of the type. The first Dakotas were taken over from the RAF in the Middle East during 1943/44 and have remained in service since. In 1992 a modification programme was announced which included the fitting of turboprop engines. A number of Dakotas are now used in the maritime reconnaissance role replacing the Shackleton and known as the 'Dackleton' and these could be supplemented by a turboprop powered maritime version. *(SAAF)*

The island of Taiwan or Formosa was conquered by the Chinese Army in 1945, but in 1949 Nationalist forces were defeated on the mainland and withdrew to Taiwan. The President, Chiang Ching-kuo, eldest son of General Chiang Kai-shek is Supreme Commander of the Armed Forces including the Chinese Nationalist Air Force – CNAF. Over 20 ex USAF C-47s have been operated by the Air Transport Wing, some wartime Lend-Lease transports supplied to China. It is believed that a handful remain in service today. Depicted is '7347' not identified and now in the CNAF museum collection.
(AP Publications)

RIGHT:
A recent survey indicates that at least a dozen C-47 transports remain in service with the Royal Thai Air Force, serving with No.603 'Cowboy' Squadron and often detached to air bases throughout Thailand. Some 60 C-47s, including AC-47 gunships, have served over the years with one VIP aircraft '76517' for use by the Thai Royal family. It is ex 44-76517 c/n 16101. Heavily camouflaged they include '789' which is ex 42-92789 c/n 12629. A dedication to the C-47 stands in front of No.603 Squadron HQ and includes the tail unit of '536' ex 42-100536 which crashed at Lunburi during 1984/5. *(Ted Kidner)*

BELOW:
Depicted at Hatzerin air base on 11 December 1989 are a couple of operational C-47 transports of the Israeli Defence Air Force (IDAF). Dakota '038' carries the radio call-sign '4X-FNZ' and '04' in the background '4X-FNL' this transport from 122 Squadron based at Ben Gurion air base, Lod. This unit operates RC-47 aircraft fitted with equipment for the Electronic Intelligence (ELINT) role. Reports suggest that between 12 and 18 Dakotas remain in IDAF service, but as the type is operational no official information can be released until five years after the last C-47 is retired. *(Peter R. Arnold)*

After World War 2 a number of surplus USAAF C-47s and C-53s were purchased by the Aeronautica Militaire Italiano (AMI) from stocks held in Naples. Depicted is C-47 MM61893 '14-46' c/n 4236 which as a DC-3 I-LINA served with Alitalia. The colourful livery was added in November 1981 when the transport was based with the Centro Radiomisure unit and used for radar calibration tasks.

With the end of World War 2 and the occupation of Western Europe and Japan there was initially an increased need for utility and general communications aircraft. With the formation of the US Air Force on 18 September 1947, new command structures were set up, with base flights utilising at least one C-47 'Gooney Bird'. Depicted is C-47 44-76671 c/n 33003 which as a VC-47D served with the 50th Tactical Fighter Wing, 17th Air Force up to April 1972. It is now in the Lackland Air Museum, San Antonio, Texas.

When the Luftwaffe was reformed in 1956 some 20 Douglas C-47s
were supplied by reverse Lend-Lease stocks from the huge surplus of
C-47s held by the USAF, most if not all being ex-RAF Dakotas
which were completely refurbished and modernised. Depicted is
'14+01' c/n 26989 ex-KK209 which was withdrawn from Luftwaffe
use on 31 March 1976. It is today in the Deutsches Museum at
Oberschleissheim, near Munich.

The Royal Danish Air Force commenced operating the military DC-3
in September 1953, when Eskadrille 721 formed utilising two ex-
SAS aircraft. During 1956 six C-47s were acquired from the Royal
Norwegian Air Force, the type being used until 1982. Depicted in
landing sequence is K-686 c/n 19475 which is now in the USA as
N54NA.

The Douglas C-47 'Gooney Bird' was given a new lease of life when
the US Air Force discovered its capabilities as a platform for
miniguns in Vietnam. It joined the modern age of electronics and
avionics with no problems. Depicted is the artwork on a AC-47
Gunship, the type used to seek out the Viet Cong after darkness
using gunfire and high powered flares. *(Robert F. Dorr)*

The Papua New Guinea Defence Force Air Transport Squadron was formed with four ex-RAAF Douglas C-47B Dakotas in 1975–6 to which two more were added later. Depicted in flight over the rugged, New Guinea coastline is Dakota P2-005 which is now civilianised in Australia along with P2-001 and P2-003. The PNGDF Dakota fleet has been replaced.

Restored to its original US Navy identity is Douglas R4D-6S
BuNo.50819 c/n 26874 registered N229GB in flying condition with
the Mid-Atlantic Air Museum, Middleton, Pennsylvania. It carries the
nose emblem of VR-2 Squadron which as part of the huge Naval Air
Transport Service (NATS) which was formed at Alameda, California
in the early days of World War 2. The pilot's name under the cockpit
is that of Jan Churchill, a very competent female pilot.

Chronology

June 1934	Bill Littlewood of American Airlines analysed possibilities of a wide-body DC-2 with R-1830-G5 engines and accommodation for 14 sleeper berths. Cyrus R. Smith (American Airlines President) made telephone call to Donald Douglas at Santa Monica, from Chicago, lasting two hours proposing order for developed DC-2 (DST). Preliminary design work began at Douglas Aircraft, Santa Monica, under Arthur E. Raymond on wide-body development of DC-2 with Wright Cyclone G-5 engines to outline requirements drawn up by Bill Littlewood and Otto Kirchner. As for the DC-1 and DC-2 the aerodynamics were under Bailey Oswald, in association with Clark B. Millikan and A.L. Klein – under Theodor von Karman, Guggenheim Aeronautics Laboratory of the Californian Institute of Technology. The layout was under Ed Burton, and stress analysis by Lee Attwood.
December '34	Manufacture began of the prototype DST.
10 May 1935	Douglas Aircraft report No.1004 set out general outline, weights, and performance of Douglas Sleeper Transport derived from DC-2 to American Airline requirements.
27 June 1935	Harry E Wetzel, wrote to Bill Littlewood quoting prices for 5, 6 or 10 DST sleeper transports for delivery at rate of one per week beginning 15 February, 1936. Subject to acceptance within 10 days and quoted prices were 5 DSTs $82,000 each, 6 DSTs $81,000 each, and 10 DSTs $79,000 each.
8 July 1935	Telegram from C.R. Smith to Douglas Aircraft stating: "Enter our order 10 model DST airplanes delivery according letter from Wetzel June 27." Telegram proposed that A.A. have rights to first 10 aircraft off the production line and weights and performance to be guaranteed in line with Douglas report No.1004.
9 July 1935	Wetzel telegraphed Smith stating that imperative details of DST arrangements and equipment be agreed immediately and suggested Littlewood fly urgently to Santa Monica.
11 July 1935	Littlewood telegraphed Wetzel that he would arrive Tuesday or Wednesday, July 16 or 17, 1935.
16 July 1935	Littlewood went to Santa Monica to discuss DC-3 with Raymond and Wetzel. Dan Beard and H.W. Beals of A.A. at Santa Monica at work on cockpit details and control forces. Beals was resident A.A. representative at Douglas Aircraft after taking delivery of last Vultee V-1A in September 1934. Beard returned to Chicago in January 1935 before going back to Santa Monica in November.
14 Dec 1935	Roll-out and first ground engine run of 1 hr 30 min of Cyclone G.5 engines in prototype DST X14988 c/n 1494. Engine run by crew chief Woolfolk.
16 Dec 1935	Second ground engine run, also of 1 hr 30 min by Woolfolk.
17 Dec 1935	Prototype DST X14988 made first flight from Clover Field flown by Carl Cover with Frank Collbohm and Ed Stineman as flight observers, and Jack Grant, mechanic. Take-off 1500 hours and landing after 30 min. Two more flights making a total of 1 hr 40 min.
18/19 Dec '36	Flight tests continued with pilots Carl Cover, Elling Veblen and Dan Beard. Bill Littlewood flew on ninth flight on 20 December, 1210-1330 hours with Dan Beard as pilot.
31 Dec 1935	By this date DST X14988 prototype had made 28 flights making total time 25 hrs 45 mins and had flown every day since 17 December, except for 21, 25 and 27 December.
1/5 Jan 1936	DST X14988 exhibited in National Pacific Aircraft & Boat Show in Los Angeles Auditorium.
6 Jan 1936	Test flying resumed at Clover Field with most flying done by Dan Beard. Tommy Tomlinson of TWA had first ride in DST with Dan Beard as pilot. Douglas had at that time only insured Beard and Veblen to fly DST.
6/10 Jan 1936	First DST X14988 flown by Dan Beard on engineering test flights 6-10 Jan inclusive. Aircraft then grounded for rest of month.
February '36	Test flying resumed on 14 February until 17th, after which aircraft grounded for double engine change and flown again 27-29 February.
17 Feb 1936	Aircraft grounded for 10 days for change of both engines. Bob Johnson and Bill Berren of Wright tuned up G.5 engines to give 1,000 hp each, compared with previous 925 hp.
March 1936	First DST flown again 3-5 March inclusive and then 23 March to the end of the month.

5 March 1936	Near accident at Mines Field, Los Angeles airport, on landing tests through brake failure. Aircraft then grounded for furnishing and fabrication of dorsal fin after completion of wind-tunnel tests by Bailey Oswald.
5/10 March	DST X14988 test flown.
8 April 1936	Contract signed between American Airlines and Douglas Aircraft for supply of aircraft from Douglas to the airline.
29 April 1936	CAA certification ATC 607 obtained for DST prototype X14988 at 24,000 lb all-up-weight. DST X14988 delivered to Phoenix, Arizona by Jake Moxness of Douglas Aircraft and formally accepted there by American Airlines to avoid Californian sales tax. Then flown back to Santa Monica by American pilots.
April 1936	United Airlines flew X14988 for full day and signed up for 20 aircraft.
2 May 1936	American Airlines began airline proving run with DST now registered NC14988. Flew Glendale to Fort Worth in 6 hrs 49 mins with pilots Dan Beard, Mitchell and Sloniger.
7 May 1936	Completion of airline proving run with flight from Douglas, Arizona to Glendale in 3 hrs 31 mins.
27/30 May '36	NC14988 grounded while 60 detailed items in dispute sorted out between American and Douglas. High level involving Donald Douglas, Arthur Raymond, Cyrus Smith, and Bill Littlewood.
27 May 1936	American cleared second DST NC16001 c/n 1495 after inspection before first flight.
4 June 1936	Second DST and first full production aircraft made its first flight.
6 June 1936	Dan Beard completed 7 hrs 44 mins of test flying in DST NC16001.
7 June 1936	Dan Beard and Elling Veblen flew NC16001 to Phoenix for American Airlines acceptance on delivery. After formal acceptance Dan Beard flew aircraft nonstop to Fort Worth, Texas.
8 June 1936	Dan Beard flew NC16001 to Dallas and then nonstop to Chicago. Aircraft was first DC-3 type to be received by American Airlines at their headquarters in Chicago, Illinois.
14 June 1936	First flight of third DST NC16002 c/n 1496 at Clover Field.
17 June 1936	NC16001 delivered to Phoenix by Elling Veblen for American acceptance. Flown from there to Chicago by airline pilots. Named at Chicago *Flagship Illinois*.
25 June 1936	Inaugural DC-3 (DST) "American Eagle" service Chicago – Newark flown by Capt. W.W. Braznell with first officer W.A. Miller with 13 passengers and Cyrus R. Smith. *Flagship Illinois* take-off 1200 EST scheduled landing 1655 EST + 3 hrs 55 mins (westbound) 4 hrs 45 mins. *"The most significant date in the first 25 years of air transport history."*
11 July 1936	First DST NC14988 handed over to American Airlines at Phoenix on completion of engine test flying.
16 Aug 1936	First flight of first 21-passenger DC-3 dayplane NC16009 c/n 1543 at Clover Field.
18 Aug 1936	NC16009 delivered to American Airlines at Phoenix and then flown to Chicago.
18 Sept 1936	Inaugural "American Mercury" overnight coast-to-coast air service both ways between Newark and Grand Central, Glendale, Los Angeles, with stops at Memphis, Dallas and Tucson. Scheduled elapsed time 15 hrs 50 min eastbound and 17 hrs 4 mins westbound.
21 Sept 1936	First export DC-3 delivered to KLM at Amsterdam, PH-ALI *Ibis* c/n 1590. Later registered G-AGBB and shot down by the Luftwaffe over Bay of Biscay on 1 June 1943.
1 Oct 1936	Second transcontinental route opened by American Airlines with DST airliners "The Southerner" was operated in both directions with four stops.
31 Dec 1936	In the year 1936 United States airlines as a whole carried 1.02 million passengers in 272 aircraft – double the number of passengers for 1934 when only 462,000 were carried. At year's end, American Airlines had in service 20 DC-3 aircraft of which 12 were 21-passenger dayplanes and eight 14-passenger DSTs, the former on New York – Boston and New York – Chicago services, the latter on transcontinental services.

By the end of 1936, a total of 63 DC-3s had been sold:

     25 to American Airlines (including eight DSTs.)
     20 to United Air Lines
     8 to KLM via Fokker
     8 to Transcontinental & Western Air (TWA)
     2 to Eastern Air Lines

By the end of 1936, a total of 31 Douglas airliners had been delivered:

     20 to American Airlines
     1 to KLM via Fokker
     10 to United Air Lines

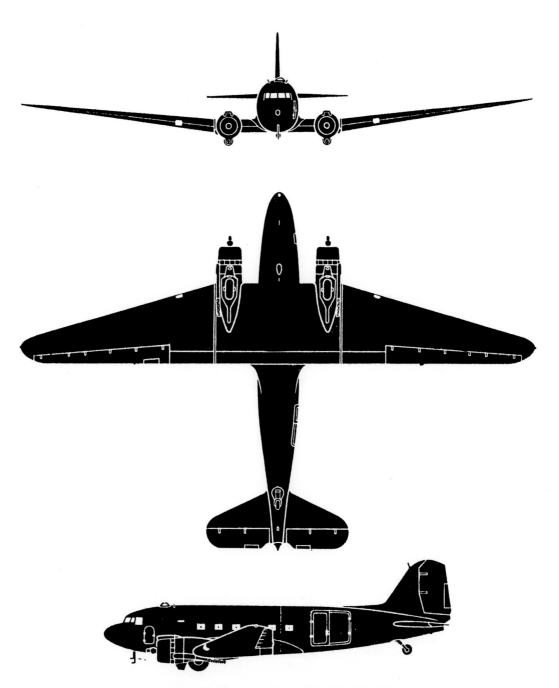

DOUGLAS DAKOTA SPECIFICATION
Powered by: Two Pratt & Whitney Twin-Wasp R.1830-90C nine-cylinder engines, each
driving a 12 ft 0 in diameter three-blade propeller.
Wing span: 95 ft 0 in. Length: 64 ft 6 in
Wing area: 987 sq ft. Gross weight: 31,000 lb
Max cruising speed: 192 mph at 10,000 ft
Max range: 2,125 nautical miles
Passenger/troops: 28

The Douglas DC-3: Family Tree

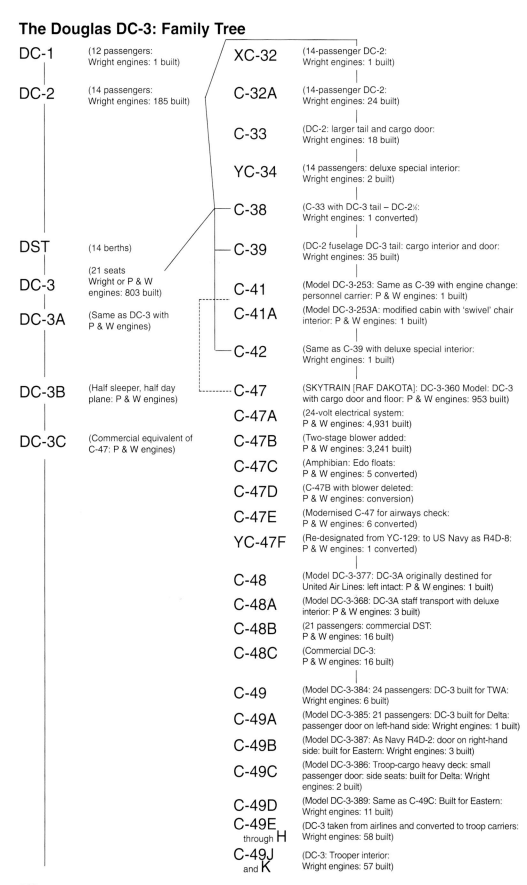

DC-1 (12 passengers: Wright engines: 1 built)

DC-2 (14 passengers: Wright engines: 185 built)

DST (14 berths)

DC-3 (21 seats Wright or P & W engines: 803 built)

DC-3A (Same as DC-3 with P & W engines)

DC-3B (Half sleeper, half day plane: P & W engines)

DC-3C (Commercial equivalent of C-47: P & W engines)

XC-32 (14-passenger DC-2: Wright engines: 1 built)

C-32A (14-passenger DC-2: Wright engines: 24 built)

C-33 (DC-2: larger tail and cargo door: Wright engines: 18 built)

YC-34 (14 passengers: deluxe special interior: Wright engines: 2 built)

C-38 (C-33 with DC-3 tail – DC-2½: Wright engines: 1 converted)

C-39 (DC-2 fuselage DC-3 tail: cargo interior and door: Wright engines: 35 built)

C-41 (Model DC-3-253: Same as C-39 with engine change: personnel carrier: P & W engines: 1 built)

C-41A (Model DC-3-253A: modified cabin with 'swivel' chair interior: P & W engines: 1 built)

C-42 (Same as C-39 with deluxe special interior: Wright engines: 1 built)

C-47 (SKYTRAIN [RAF DAKOTA]: DC-3-360 Model: DC-3 with cargo door and floor: P & W engines: 953 built)

C-47A (24-volt electrical system: P & W engines: 4,931 built)

C-47B (Two-stage blower added: P & W engines: 3,241 built)

C-47C (Amphibian: Edo floats: P & W engines: 5 converted)

C-47D (C-47B with blower deleted: P & W engines: conversion)

C-47E (Modernised C-47 for airways check: P & W engines: 6 converted)

YC-47F (Re-designated from YC-129: to US Navy as R4D-8: P & W engines: 1 converted)

C-48 (Model DC-3-377: DC-3A originally destined for United Air Lines: left intact: P & W engines: 1 built)

C-48A (Model DC-3-368: DC-3A staff transport with deluxe interior: P & W engines: 3 built)

C-48B (21 passengers: commercial DST: P & W engines: 16 built)

C-48C (Commercial DC-3: P & W engines: 16 built)

C-49 (Model DC-3-384: 24 passengers: DC-3 built for TWA: Wright engines: 6 built)

C-49A (Model DC-3-385: 21 passengers: DC-3 built for Delta: passenger door on left-hand side: Wright engines: 1 built)

C-49B (Model DC-3-387: As Navy R4D-2: door on right-hand side: built for Eastern: Wright engines: 3 built)

C-49C (Model DC-3-386: Troop-cargo heavy deck: small passenger door: side seats: built for Delta: Wright engines: 2 built)

C-49D (Model DC-3-389: Same as C-49C: Built for Eastern: Wright engines: 11 built)

C-49E through H (DC-3 taken from airlines and converted to troop carriers: Wright engines: 58 built)

C-49J and K (DC-3: Trooper interior: Wright engines: 57 built)

158

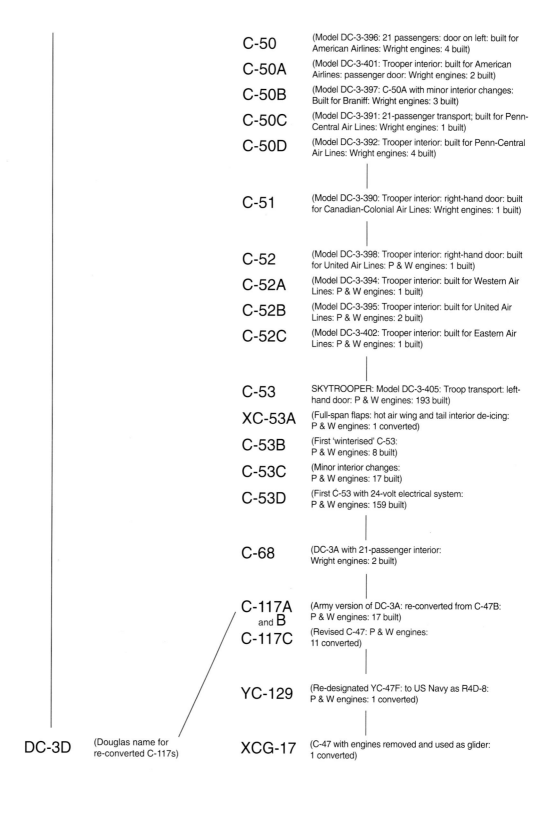

C-50 — (Model DC-3-396: 21 passengers: door on left: built for American Airlines: Wright engines: 4 built)

C-50A — (Model DC-3-401: Trooper interior: built for American Airlines: passenger door: Wright engines: 2 built)

C-50B — (Model DC-3-397: C-50A with minor interior changes: Built for Braniff: Wright engines: 3 built)

C-50C — (Model DC-3-391: 21-passenger transport; built for Penn-Central Air Lines: Wright engines: 1 built)

C-50D — (Model DC-3-392: Trooper interior: built for Penn-Central Air Lines: Wright engines: 4 built)

C-51 — (Model DC-3-390: Trooper interior: right-hand door: built for Canadian-Colonial Air Lines: Wright engines: 1 built)

C-52 — (Model DC-3-398: Trooper interior: right-hand door: built for United Air Lines: P & W engines: 1 built)

C-52A — (Model DC-3-394: Trooper interior: built for Western Air Lines: P & W engines: 1 built)

C-52B — (Model DC-3-395: Trooper interior: built for United Air Lines: P & W engines: 2 built)

C-52C — (Model DC-3-402: Trooper interior: built for Eastern Air Lines: P & W engines: 1 built)

C-53 — SKYTROOPER: Model DC-3-405: Troop transport: left-hand door: P & W engines: 193 built)

XC-53A — (Full-span flaps: hot air wing and tail interior de-icing: P & W engines: 1 converted)

C-53B — (First 'winterised' C-53: P & W engines: 8 built)

C-53C — (Minor interior changes: P & W engines: 17 built)

C-53D — (First C-53 with 24-volt electrical system: P & W engines: 159 built)

C-68 — (DC-3A with 21-passenger interior: Wright engines: 2 built)

C-117A and B — (Army version of DC-3A: re-converted from C-47B: P & W engines: 17 built)

C-117C — (Revised C-47: P & W engines: 11 converted)

YC-129 — (Re-designated YC-47F: to US Navy as R4D-8: P & W engines: 1 converted)

DC-3D — (Douglas name for re-converted C-117s)

XCG-17 — (C-47 with engines removed and used as glider: 1 converted)

Perfect propeller synchronisation seen on an RAF Dakota from its
two Pratt & Whitney Twin Wasp R-1830-92 engines. This is
registered G-DAKS c/n 19347 ex-TS423 which is often operated on
film work in different guises and owned by Aces High Limited and
based at North Weald, Essex.

Key to Douglas Dakota IV Cutaway Drawing

1 Hinged nose cone, access to instruments and controls
2 Rudder pedals
3 Instrument panel
4 Windscreen de-icing fluid spray nozzle
5 Starboard propeller
6 Windscreen panels
7 Co-pilot's seat
8 Engine throttles
9 Control column
10 Cockpit floor level
11 Access panels to control cable runs
12 Pitot static tubes
13 Aerial cables
14 Propeller de-icing fluid tank
15 Pilot's seat
16 Cockpit bulkhead
17 Cockpit roof escape hatch
18 Whip aerial
19 Starboard landing/taxiing lamp
20 Windscreen de-icing fluid tank
21 Starboard baggage compartment
22 Electrical fuse panel
23 Crew entry door
24 ADF loop aerial housing
25 Life raft stowage
26 Port baggage compartment
27 Main cabin bulkhead
28 Radio operator's seat
29 Air scoop
30 Heating and ventilating system heat exchangers
31 Astrodome observation hatch
32 Starboard outer wing panel
33 Pneumatic leading-edge de-icing boot
34 Starboard navigation light
35 Starboard aileron
36 Aileron cable controls
37 Trim tab
38 Trim tab control gear
39 Flap control shaft
40 Starboard outer flap
41 Fuselage frame and stringer construction
42 Centre fuselage main frames
43 Centre wing section corrugated inner skin
44 Port main fuel tank
45 Port auxiliary fuel tank
46 Wing spar attachments
47 Flap hydraulic jack
48 Centre section flap
49 Floor beam construction
50 Cabin window panels
51 Window panel grommets for small arms attachments
52 Paratroop seating, 28 paratroops
53 Port emergency exit window
54 Starboard emergency exit window
55 Cabin lining panels
56 Overhead heating and ventilating duct
57 Rear cabin frames
58 Fuselage skin plating
59 Rear cabin bulkhead
60 First aid kit
61 Access door to tail controls
62 Fin root fillet
63 Starboard tailplane
64 Starboard elevator
65 Fin leading-edge pneumatic de-icing boot
66 Fin construction
67 Aerial cables
68 Rudder aerodynamic balance
69 Hinge post
70 Rudder construction
71 Fabric covering
72 Rudder trim tab
73 Trim tab control gear
74 Rudder and elevator control horns
75 Fuselage tail fairing
76 Elevator trim tab
77 Port elevator construction
78 Fabric covered elevator
79 Leading-edge pneumatic de-icing boot
80 Tailplane construction
81 Tailplane attachment joint
82 Rudder stop cables
83 Tailplane centre section
84 Tailwheel
85 Shock absorber leg strut
86 Tailwheel mounting plate
87 Tailwheel strut
88 Rudder and elevator control cables
89 Tail fuselage joint frame
90 Toilet
91 Rear freight door
92 Forward freight door
93 Paratroop/passenger door
94 Fuselage stringer construction
95 Freight floor
96 Wing root trailing-edge fillet
97 Inboard split trailing-edge flap
98 Flap shroud construction
99 Fuel filler caps
100 Outer wing panel bolted joint
101 Wing panel joint capping strip
102 Outer split trailing-edge flap
103 Port aileron
104 Aileron fabric covering
105 Detachable wing tip joint rib
106 Port navigation light
107 Leading-edge pneumatic de-icing boot
108 Wing stringer construction
109 Rear spar
110 Centre spar
111 Wing rib construction
112 Wing rib
113 Leading-edge nose ribs
114 Leading-edge stringers
115 Port landing/taxiing lamp
116 Port mainwheel
117 Main undercarriage rear strut
118 Shock absorber leg struts
119 Undercarriage knee joints
120 Exhaust pipe
121 Undercarriage bungee cables
122 Engine nacelle fairing
123 Oil tank
124 Undercarriage retraction jack
125 Mainwheel well
126 Engine fireproof bulkhead
127 Engine bearer struts
128 Oil cooler
129 Cooling air exit flaps
130 Exhaust collector pipe
131 Engine air intake
132 Engine cowlings
133 Pratt & Whitney R-1830-90C air-cooled 14-cylinder, radial engine
134 Propeller hub pitch change mechanism
135 Hamilton Standard constant speed three-bladed propeller

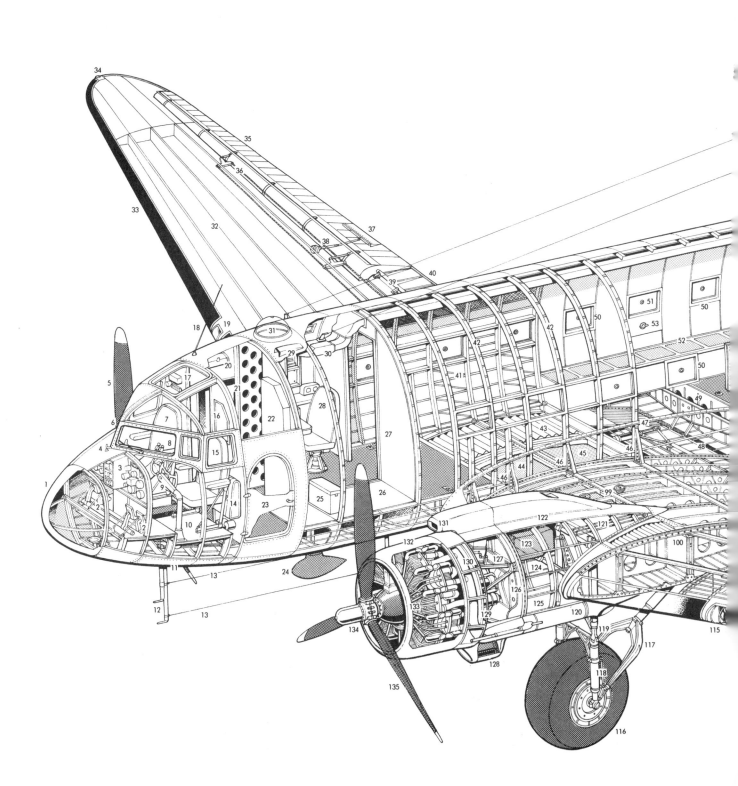